LABORATORY MANUAL TO ACCOMPANY

Fundamentals of Communications and Networking

World Headquarters
Jones & Bartlett Learning
5 Wall Street
Burlington, MA 01803
978-443-5000
info@jblearning.com
www.jblearning.com

Jones & Bartlett Learning books and products are available through most bookstores and online booksellers. To contact Jones & Bartlett Learning directly, call 800-832-0034, fax 978-443-8000, or visit our website, www.jblearning.com.

Substantial discounts on bulk quantities of Jones & Bartlett Learning publications are available to corporations, professional associations, and other qualified organizations. For details and specific discount information, contact the special sales department at Jones & Bartlett Learning via the above contact information or send an email to specialsales@jblearning.com.

Production Credits
Chief Executive Officer: Ty Field
President: James Homer
SVP, Chief Technology Officer: Dean Fossella
SVP, Chief Marketing Officer: Alison M. Pendergast
SVP, Curriculum Solutions: Christopher Will
VP, Design and Production: Anne Spencer
VP, Manufacturing and Inventory Control: Therese Connell
Author: vLab Solutions, LLC, David Kim, President
Editorial Management: Perspectives, Inc., Phil Graham, President
Reprints and Special Projects Manager: Susan Schultz
Associate Production Editor: Tina Chen
Director of Marketing: Alisha Weisman
Senior Marketing Manager: Andrea DeFronzo
Cover Design: Anne Spencer
Composition: vLab Solutions, LLC
Cover Image: © Oriontrail/ShutterStock, Inc.
Printing and Binding: Malloy, Inc.
Cover Printing: Malloy, Inc.

ISBN: 978-1-4496-7134-1

6048
Printed in the United States of America
15 14 13 12   10 9 8 7 6 5 4 3

Table of Contents

Current Version Date: 10/10/2011

Laboratory #1

Lab 1: Cisco Router / Switch Hardware & Software Discovery

Learning Objectives and Outcomes

Upon completing this lab, students will be able to:

- Establish a remote TELNET connection to a Cisco device using PuTTy

- Enter various show commands to document the router / switch model, RAM, IOS version, and configuration register settings

- Enter various show commands to display and capture the router / switch inventory and hardware interfaces

- Perform an emergency password recovery of a Cisco router / switch

- Make a back-up copy of the Cisco router /switch device's current running config file by TFTP-ing to a TFTP server

Required Setup and Tools

This course requires the use of the Onsite "Mock" IT Infrastructure and virtualized server farm. This is shown below:

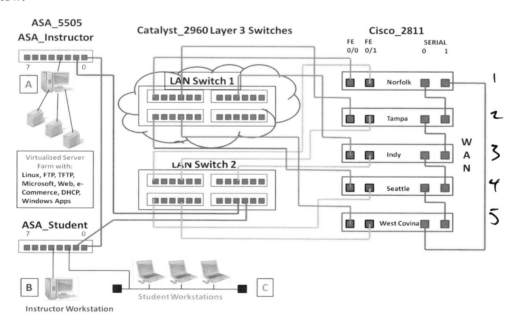

Figure 1 – Standard Onsite "Mock" IT Infrastructure & Virtualized Server Farm

Current Version Date: 10/10/2011

The "Mock" IT Infrastructure is a preconfigured, IP network infrastructure complete with a classroom virtualized server farm. All IP addressing schema, VLAN configurations, and layer 3 switching is preconfigured. The IP networking infrastructure remains static and includes the following removable parts as indicated in Figure 1 above:

A) **NEEDED** – A classroom workstation (with at least 4 Gig RAM) capable of supporting an insert-able hard drive or USB hard drive with a preconfigured, virtualized server farm. This classroom workstation will support the virtualized VM server farm connected to the ASA_Instructor VLAN.

B) **NEEDED** – An "Instructor VM" workstation (with at least 2 Gig RAM) that shall act as the demonstration traffic generator for the protocol capture of equipment-based labs. The Instructor will engage ARP, DHCP, ICMP, TCP 3-way handshake, FTP, HTTP, TELNET, and SSH to demonstrate protocol interaction from a preconfigured Instructor Virtual Machine (VM). The Instructor workstation/server connects to the "ASA_Student" on any of the available ports to mimic the Student's configuration. These available ports are configured to be on the same logical VLAN; hence, any port can be used. The student lab workstations connect to the same "ASA_Student" on any of the available ports.

C) **NEEDED** – "Student VM" workstations (with at least 2 Gig RAM) use a preconfigured "Student VM" to act as an Attacker VM as well as a traffic monitoring and protocol capture device. Since all the ports on the "ASA_Student" are on the same VLAN, student workstations must connect to any of the ports on the ASA5505. Students must capture the protocol interaction by generating their own unique attack traffic to their target VM in order to answer Lab #1 - Assessment Worksheet questions.

The following summarizes the setup, configuration, and equipment needed to perform Lab #1:

- Standard Onsite "Mock" IT Infrastructure configuration and setup
  - Cisco 28xx routers, 29xx catalyst LAN switches, and ASA 5505 firewalls
  - TELNET accessible Cisco routers, SSH accessible Cisco routers, ICMP enabled on Cisco routers
- A virtualized server farm with:
  - A Microsoft Server VM for DHCP and other required network services
  - A Student and/or "Instructor VM" to use as the "Attacker VM" and traffic monitor

Current Version Date: 10/10/2011

- A "Target VM" Microsoft and/or Linux Server with the following:
    - Sample Website supporting HTTP and/or HTTPS
  - FTP and TFTP services enabled
- TCP/IP protocol primer cheat sheet with well-known port numbers (Included at the end of the lab manual.)
- Standard onsite Instructor and "Student VM" must have the following software applications loaded to perform this lab:
  - VMWare Player
- Standard Instructor and "Student VM" will be preconfigured with the following software:
  - Wireshark 1.2.9 for packet capturing and protocol analysis
  - NetWitness Investigator v 9.0 for packet capturing and protocol analysis
  - TELNET and SSH open source client software – PuTTY
  - FTP and TFTP open source client software – FileZilla and TFTPd32
  - Adobe Reader for PDF Documentation
  - Microsoft Word for Lab Assessment Worksheet Questions & Answers

Equipment-Based Lab #1 – Student Steps:

Students should perform the following steps:

1. Insert your student removable hard drive or USB hard drive into a classroom workstation with VMWare Player pre-loaded
2. Boot up the "Student VM" workstation ("Student VM")
3. Log into your Student VM
4. Engage the command prompt on the "Student VM" and PING various IP hosts, Cisco router interfaces, and LAN switch ports on this IP subnetwork: (Zenmap Gui scan of 172.30.0.0/24)
5. Run the PuTTY application from the "Student VM" and enter the targeted IP address of a network device (ASA Security Devices, LAN Switches or Location Routers, your choice)
6. Once connected to a device, hit the "ENTER" key to get started.
7. Once at the Terminal console password prompt enter the password "cisco" and hit the "ENTER" key, the Router/Switch prompt will appear.

Current Version Date: 10/10/2011

8. Enter the command "show version" at the prompt. Figure 2 below shows an example of the "show version" command at work and the information it reveals concerning the specific network device you are connected to.

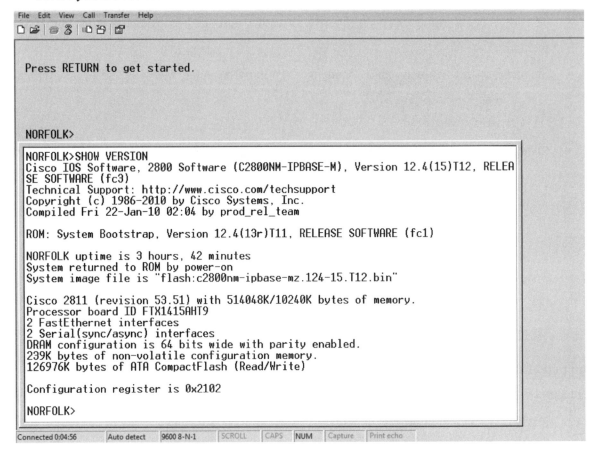

Figure 2 – Show Version Command Display

9. From the information displayed determine the following information and complete the Lab #1-Supplement Sheet, Cisco Router Hardware & Software Discovery Table provided below for each device.

    *   The Router/Switch Model Number.

    *   The RAM.

    *   The IOS Software Version.

    *   The Configuration Register hexadecimal value.

    *   The total amount of physical interfaces.

Current Version Date: 10/10/2011

Equipment-Based Lab #1 – Student Steps:

Students should perform the following steps:

1. Insert your student removable hard drive or USB hard drive into a classroom workstation with VMWare Player pre-loaded.

2. Boot up the "Student VM" workstation ("Student VM") and log into your Student VM.

3. Select a target IP address on one of the location router's Fast Ethernet ports and record it.

4. Run the PuTTY application from the "Student VM" workstation and log into the Location router for which you recorded the IP address for the Fast Ethernet port.

5. Once connected to the Location Router for which you recorded the IP address, hit the "ENTER" key to get started.

6. Turn-on the TFTPd32 application on the "Student VM" workstation

7. Make sure the IP host address of the "Student VM" workstation is displayed correctly in the HOST ID field of TFTPd32 application.

8. PING both IP addresses to confirm IP connectivity between the FastEthernet0/0 interface (Router#> ping command) and "Instructor VM" workstation (in DOS command line, c:\> ping command)

9. At the Router> prompt, issue the "enable" command, and provide the password "cisco" when prompted.

10. The prompt changes to Router#, which indicates that the router is now in privileged mode.

11. To copy the running configuration file to the TFTP server type the following at the Router# prompt "copy running-config tftp".

12. At the address/name of remote host insert the "Instructor VM" workstation host IP address (172.16.xx.xx)

13. Issue a name for the file eg "backup_running_config" and hit ENTER.

14. Browse to the saved file location on the "Student VM" in the TFTP directory.

15. Submit saved file to you instructor labeled

    "*YourName*_LAB1_backdup_running_config_lastnamefirst initial" to you instructor along with you completed Lab #1 Assessment Questions

Deliverables

Upon completion of the Cisco Router Hardware & Software Discovery Lab, students are required to provide the following deliverables:

Current Version Date: 10/10/2011

1. A completed Cisco Hardware & Software Discovery Device Table for all devices on the Cisco Backbone Network.

2. A softcopy of the "backup_running_config" file emailed to the instructor.

3. Lab #1 - Assessment Worksheet with answers to the assessment questions

Evaluation Criteria and Rubrics

The following are the evaluation criteria and rubrics for Lab #1 that the students must perform:

1. Was the student able to establish a remote TELNET connection to a Cisco device using PuTTy? - **[20%]**

2. Was the student successfully able to enter various show commands to document the router / switch model, RAM, IOS version, and configuration register settings? - **[20%]**

3. Was the student able to successfully enter various show commands to display and capture the router / switch inventory and hardware interfaces? - **[20%]**

4. Was the student able to successfully perform an emergency password recovery of a Cisco router / switch? - **[20%]**

5. Was the student able to make a back-up copy of the Cisco router /switch device's current running configuration file by TFTP-ing to a TFTP server? - **[20%]**

Current Version Date: 10/10/2011

Lab #1 – Supplement Sheet

Mock IT Infrastructure IP Addressing Schema

		Mock IT Infrastructure IP Address Chart			
Router Name	**Serial 0/0**	**Serial 0/1**	**Fastethernet 0/0**	**Fastethernet 0/1**	**Loopback 0**
R1.WEST COVINA	172.19.0.2 /30	172.20.0.1 /30	172.20.8.1 /24	172.20.20.1 /24	172.20.1.1 /32
Description	R1.SEATTLE-S 0/1	R1.NORFOLK-S 0/1	DMZ-LAN-SW1-FE0/16	TRUST-LAN-SW2-FE0/16	
Router Name	**Serial 0/0**	**Serial 0/1**	**Fastethernet 0/0**	**Fastethernet 0/1**	**Loopback 0**
R1.SEATTLE	172.18.0.2 /30	172.19.0.1 /30	172.19.8.1 /24	172.19.20.1 /24	172.19.1.1 /32
Description	R1.INDY-S 0/1	R1.WESTCOVINA-S 0/0	DMZ-LAN-SW1-F0/2-V400	TRUST-LAN-SW2-F0/2-V401	
Router Name	**Serial 0/0**	**Serial 0/1**	**Fastethernet 0/0**	**Fastethernet 0/1**	**Loopback 0**
R1.INDY	172.17.0.2 /30	172.18.0.1 /30	172.18.8.1 /24	172.18.20.1 /24	172.18.1.1 /32
Description	R1.TAMPA-S 0/1	R1.SEATTLE-S 0/0	DMZ-LAN-SW1-F0/17-V300	TRUST-LAN-SW2-F0/17-V301	
Router Name	**Serial 0/0**	**Serial 0/1**	**Fastethernet 0/0**	**Fastethernet 0/1**	**Loopback 0**
R1.TAMPA	172.16.0.2 /30	172.17.0.1 /30	172.17.8.1 /24	172.17.20.1 /24	172.17.1.1 /32
Description	R1.NORFOLK-S 0/1	R1.INDY-S 0/0	DMZ-LAN-SW1-F0/7-V200	TRUST-LAN-SW2-F0/7-V201	
Router Name	**Serial 0/0**	**Serial 0/1**	**Fastethernet 0/0**	**Fastethernet 0/1**	**Loopback 0**
R1.NORFOLK	172.20.0.2 /30	172.16.0.1 /30	172.16.8.1 /24	172.16.20.1 /24	172.16.1.1 /32
Description	R1.WEST COVINA-S 0/1	R1.TAMPA-S 0/0	DMZ-LAN-SW1-FE0/1	TRUST-LAN-SW2-FE0/1	
Switch Name	**Vlan 100**	**Fastethernet 0/1**	**Fastethernet 0/2**	**Fastethernet 0/7**	**Fastethernet 0/8**
LAN.SW1	172.16.8.5 /24				
Description		R1.NORFOLK-F 0/0	R1.SEATTLE-F 0/0	R1.TAMPA-F0/0	R1.WEST COVINA-F0/0
Switch Name	**Vlan 101**	**Fastethernet 0/1**	**Fastethernet 0/2**	**Fastethernet 0/7**	**Fastethernet 0/8**
LAN.SW2	172.16.20.5 /24				
Description		R1.NORFOLK-F 0/1	R1.SEATTLE-F 0/1	R1.TAMPA-F0/1	R1.WEST COVINA-F0/1
ASA Name	**Vlan2 "Inside"**	**Vlan501 "Outside"**	**Vlan600 "DMZ"**		
ASA-Student	172.31.0.1 /24 (IP Default GW)	172.20.20.10 /24	172.29.0.2 /24		
Description	Can only ping this from vlan2.	Can ping this from outside.	Cannot ping this from outside.		
ASA Name	**Vlan2 "Inside"**	**Vlan501 "Outside"**	**Vlan600 "DMZ"**		
ASA-Instructor	172.30.0.1 /24 (IP Default GW)	172.20.20.11 /24	172.29.0.1 /24		
Description	Can ony ping this from vlan2.	Can ping this from outside.	Cannot ping this from outside.		

Lab #1 – Supplement Sheet

Cisco Router Hardware & Software Discovery Table

CISCO HARDWARE & SOFTWARE DISCOVERY DEVICE TABLE				
ASA INSTRUCTOR	Router Model RAM Flash IOS Version Configuration Register			
	Physical Ports	Ethernet		
ASA STUDENT	Router Model RAM Flash IOS Version Configuration Register			
	Physical Ports	Ethernet		
LAN SWITCH 1	Router Model RAM Flash IOS Version Configuration Register			
	Physical Ports	Ethernet		
LAN SWITCH 2	Router Model RAM Flash IOS Version Configuration Register			
	Physical Ports	Ethernet		
NORFOLK	Router Model RAM Flash IOS Version Configuration Register			
	Physical Ports	Ethernet Serial VPN Module		
TAMPA	Router Model RAM Flash IOS Version Configuration Register			
	Physical Ports	Ethernet Serial VPN Module		
INDY	Router Model RAM Flash IOS Version Configuration Register			
	Physical Ports	Ethernet Serial VPN Module		
SEATTLE	Router Model RAM Flash IOS Version Configuration Register			
	Physical Ports	Ethernet Serial VPN Module		
WEST COVINA	Router Model RAM Flash IOS Version Configuration Register			
	Physical Ports	Ethernet Serial VPN Module		

Current Version Date: 10/10/2011

Lab #1 – Assessment Worksheet

Cisco Router Hardware & Software Discovery

Course Name: _____

Student Name: _____

Instructor Name: _____

Lab Due Date: _____

Overview

In this lab, students will become familiar with the Cisco devices used in the Mock IT Infrastructure. Cisco 28xx routers, Cisco 29xx switches, and Cisco ASA 5505s will be examined and documented as part of Lab #1. In addition, the Instructor will demonstrate the back-door password recovery steps on a Cisco 28xx router for students. Students will make a back-up copy of their router / switch configuration file using as TFTP server and TELNET console connection.

Lab Assessment Questions & Answers

1. What Cisco "show" command displays various information and details about the router or switch such as Model #, flash memory, RAM, IOS version and physical interfaces?

2. During the Instructor's TELNET session to LAN Switch 1 and LAN Switch 2 – what was the captured terminal password for LAN Switch 1 and LAN Switch 2?

3. What is the size of the IOS file used for the Cisco 28xx Routers?

4. What is the command used to enter the global configuration mode for interfaces on a Cisco Router or Switch?

5. The default hexadecimal value of the configuration register setting for the Cisco 28xx Router is?

6. What are the specific settings for the configuration hexadecimal value 0x2102?

7. What is the key sequence used to interrupt the boot sequence of a router and initiate the password recovery sequence?

8. Using the password recovery process how can you break the router boot sequence to see the router saved passwords and what can you do in that mode.

9. What is the command used to back up the running-config file to TFTP?

10. What process takes place if the command "copy tftp running-config" is entered?

Current Version Date: 10/10/2011

Laboratory #2

Lab 2: IEEE 802.3 CSMA/CD & Ethernet II Networking

Learning Objectives and Outcomes

Upon completing this lab, students will be able to:

- Distinguish between protocols that use IEEE 802.3 and Ethernet II.

- Capture and inspect IEEE 802.3 and Ethernet II frames using Wireshark.

- Distinguish the differences between 802.3 and Ethernet II frame formats.

- Observe the differences in various transfer speeds of Ethernet Networking.

- Identify the differences between Hub/ Single Broadcast Domains and Switch/Multiple Broadcast Domains.

Required Setup and Tools

This course requires the use of the Onsite "Mock" IT Infrastructure and virtualized server farm. This is shown below:

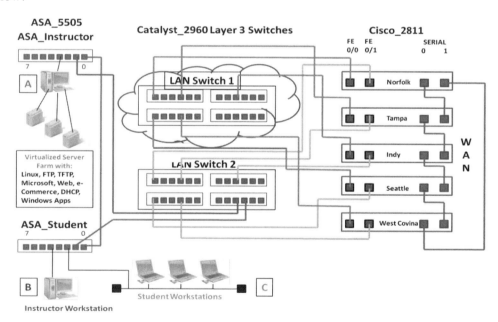

Figure 1 – Standard Onsite "Mock" IT Infrastructure & Virtualized Server Farm

Current Version Date: 10/10/2011

The "Mock" IT Infrastructure is a preconfigured, IP network infrastructure complete with a classroom virtualized server farm. All IP addressing schema, VLAN configurations, and layer 3 switching is preconfigured. The IP networking infrastructure remains static and includes the following removable parts as indicated in Figure 1 above:

A) **NEEDED** – A classroom workstation (with at least 4 Gig RAM) capable of supporting an insert-able hard drive or USB hard drive with a preconfigured, virtualized server farm. This classroom workstation will support the virtualized VM server farm connected to the ASA_Instructor VLAN.

B) **NEEDED** – An "Instructor VM" workstation (with at least 2 Gig RAM) that shall act as the demonstration traffic generator for the protocol capture of equipment-based labs. The Instructor will engage ARP, DHCP, ICMP, TCP 3-way handshake, FTP, HTTP, TELNET, and SSH to demonstrate protocol interaction from a preconfigured Instructor Virtual Machine (VM). The Instructor workstation/server connects to the "ASA_Student" on any of the available ports to mimic the Student's configuration. These available ports are configured to be on the same logical VLAN; hence, any port can be used. The student lab workstations connect to the same "ASA_Student" on any of the available ports.

C) **NEEDED** – "Student VM" workstations (with at least 2 Gig RAM) use a preconfigured "Student VM" to act as an Attacker VM as well as a traffic monitoring and protocol capture device. Since all the ports on the "ASA_Student" are on the same VLAN, student workstations must connect to any of the ports on the ASA5505. Students must capture the protocol interaction by generating their own unique attack traffic to their target VM in order to answer Lab #2 - Assessment Worksheet questions.

The following summarizes the setup, configuration, and equipment needed to perform Lab #2:

- Standard Onsite "Mock" IT Infrastructure configuration and setup
  - Cisco 28xx routers, 29xx catalyst LAN switches, and ASA 5505 firewalls
  - TELNET accessible Cisco routers, SSH accessible Cisco routers, ICMP enabled on Cisco routers
- A virtualized server farm with:
  - A Microsoft Server VM for DHCP and other required network services
  - A Student and/or "Instructor VM" to use as the "Attacker VM" and traffic monitor
  - A "Target VM" Microsoft and/or Linux Server with the following:

Current Version Date: 10/10/2011

- Sample Website supporting HTTP and/or HTTPS
  - FTP and TFTP services enabled
- TCP/IP protocol primer cheat sheet with well-known port numbers (Included at the end of the lab manual.)
- Standard onsite Instructor and "Student VM" must have the following software applications loaded to perform this lab:
  - VMWare Player
- Standard Instructor and "Student VM" will be preconfigured with the following software:
  - Wireshark 1.2.9 for packet capturing and protocol analysis
  - TELNET and SSH open source client software – PuTTY
  - FTP and TFTP open source client software – FileZilla and TFTPd32
  - Adobe Reader for PDF Documentation
  - Microsoft Word for Lab Assessment Worksheet Questions & Answers

Equipment-Based Lab #2 – Student Steps:

Students should perform the following steps:

1. Insert your Student removable hard drive or USB hard drive to a classroom workstation
2. Start the VMWare Player application on the classroom workstation
3. Boot up and log into your Student VM.
4. Turn on Wireshark on the "Student VM" and begin a new packet capturing sequence.
5. Engage the command prompt on the "Instructor VM" and PING various IP hosts, Cisco router interfaces, and LAN switch ports.
6. Launch a new browser window in Internet Explorer and navigate to any three (3) websites (attempt logging in to Hotmail, Gmail, run a Youtube video sequence, etc.)
7. Exit the browser and stop the Wireshark capture sequence and save the file as "*YourName* Lab#2 IP capture".
8. Navigate to the "*YourName* Lab#2 IP capture" file and reopen it using Wireshark.
9. On the Wireshark interface move the pointer to the "Analyze" tab then click on "Enabled Protocols"

Current Version Date: 10/10/2011

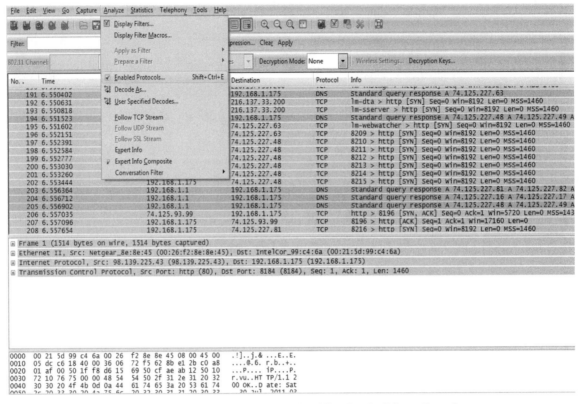

Figure 6 - Navigate to Analyze in Wiresharks Menu Interface

10. Select the "Disable All" button located at the bottom of the window, in the "Protocol" window scroll to "IP" check the box and click "OK"

11. Wireshark will filter the capture file to show only packets with the IP protocol.

12. Select an IP packet frame and inspect the characteristics of the frame for Ethernet II encapsulation

13. Return to the "Enable Protocols" section and re-enable all.

Current Version Date: 10/10/2011

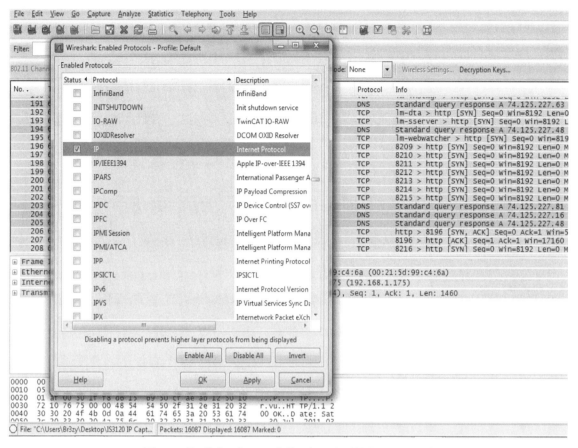

Figure 7 - Selecting and Setting the IP Protocol Filter

14. Redo steps 9 - 12, for Step 14 select "CDP" instead of "IP" in the "Protocol" window

15. Select a CDP packet and inspect the characteristics of the frame for IEEE 802.3 encapsulation.

Current Version Date: 10/10/2011

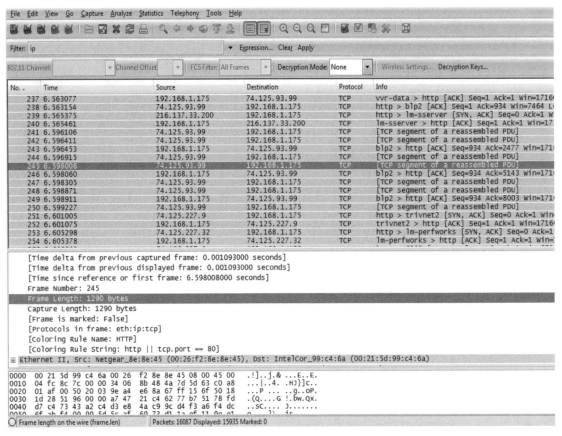

Figure 8 - Frame Analysis Window

16. Determine the differences in length and layout of the two packets. Create screenshots of the two packets and submit them with the capture file to your Instructor. (Refer to the frame analysis below for encapsulation characteristics and differences)

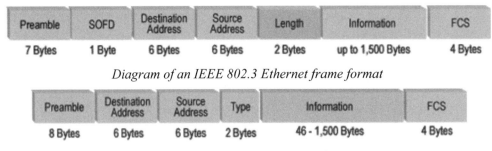

Diagram of an IEEE 802.3 Ethernet frame format

Diagram of an EthernetV2 frame format

Current Version Date: 10/10/2011

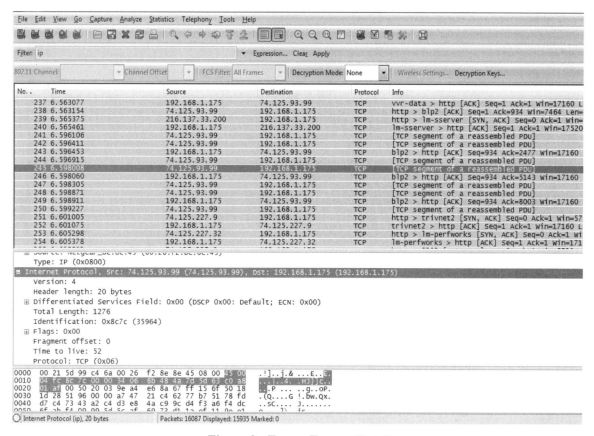

Figure 9 - Frame Format Details

17. On the "Student VM" create a TFTpd32 connection to the "TargetWindows01" VM using the
    TFTpd32 application.

18. Your instructor will provide you with the IP address of the "TargetWindows01" VM.

19. On your "Student VM", navigate to the LAN connection in Control Panel.

20. Right click on the connection icon and select "Properties", click on "Configure" and select the
    "Advanced" tab.

Current Version Date: 10/10/2011

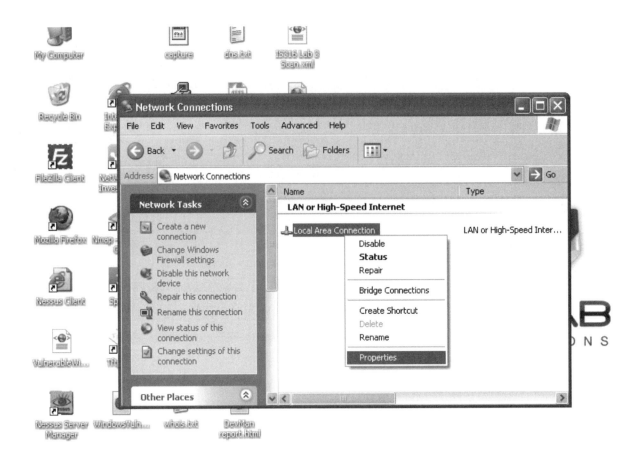

Figure 10 - LAN Connection Properties

21. Under the "Properties" window, highlight "External PHY" and change the "Value" setting to "10Mbps Full Duplex".

22. Attempt to retrieve the file using the "Get" command in the TFTpd32 interface and notate the average time for the transfers.

23. Repeat Steps 19 - 21 changing the setting from "10Mbps Full Duplex" to "100Mbps Full Duplex" and compare the transfer times for the different speeds.

Current Version Date: 10/10/2011

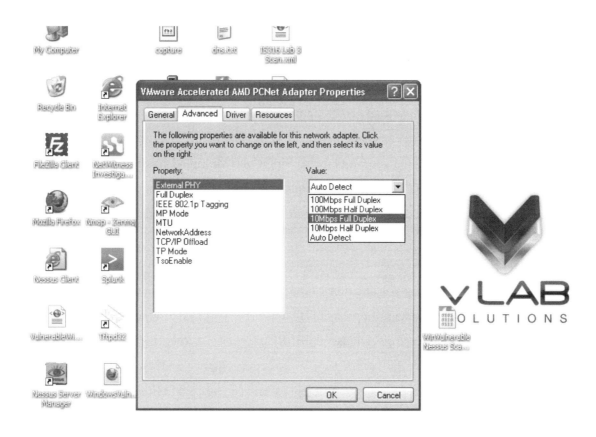

Figure 11 - Selecting the Various Transfer Speeds

24. When the exercise is complete restore original LAN connection settings.

25. Move on to Lab #2 Scenario, Identifying Hub/Single & Switch/Multiple Broadcast Domains, located at the end of the lab and complete the exercise.

Current Version Date: 10/10/2011

Deliverables

Upon completion of IEEE 802.3 CSMA/CD & Ethernet II Networking Lab, students are required to provide the following deliverables as part of this lab:

1. A softcopy of the "*YourName* Lab #2 IP Capture" Wireshark pcap file.
2. Screenshots of the packet encapsulation analysis of the Ethernet II and Ethernet 802.3 frames.
3. The Lab #2 Scenario diagram showing labeled Single and Multiple Broadcast domains accompanied by a Word Document with reasons to support your answers.
4. Lab #2 - Assessment Worksheet with answers to the assessment questions.

Evaluation Criteria and Rubrics

The following are the evaluation criteria and rubrics for Lab #2 that the students must perform:

1. Was the student able to distinguish protocols that use IEEE 802.3 and Ethernet II? - **[20%]**
2. Was the student able to Capture and inspect IEEE 802.3 and Ethernet II frames using Wireshark? - **[20%]**
3. Was the student able to distinguish the differences between 802.3 and Ethernet II frame formats? - **[20%]**
4. Was the student able to observe the differences in various transfer speeds of Ethernet Networking? - **[20%]**
5. Was the student able to identify the differences between Hub/ Single Broadcast Domains and Switch/Multiple Broadcast Domains? - **[20%]**

Current Version Date: 10/10/2011

Lab #2 Scenario

Identifying Hub/Single & Switch/Multiple Broadcast Domains

The Lab #2 Diagram below shows the network infrastructure of an organization. The network contains the following segments:

- A DMZ (Demilitarized Zone) consisting of Web, Emails and E-Commerce Servers

- 1 Gateway Router

- ISP Link

- 1 External Firewall

- 2 LAN Switches

- 2 Network Hubs

- 3 VLAN's (Virtual Local Area Networks)

- 2 Local Area Networks

Current Version Date: 10/10/2011

LAB #2 IP SINGLE & MULTIPLE BROADCAST DOMAINS

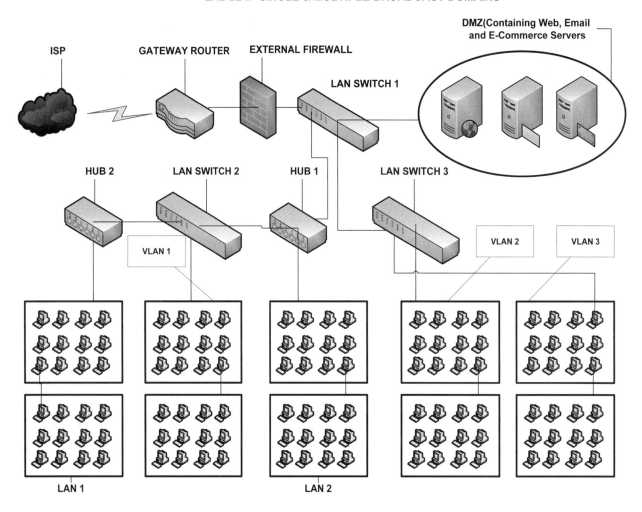

On the diagram identify and label Single and Multiple Broadcast Domains within the network infrastructure. Document reasons to support your answers on a Word Document formatted in Times New Roman, Size 12 pt, double-spaced and submit to your instructor along with your copy of the labeled segmented diagram and Lab#2 Assessment Questions Sheet.

Current Version Date: 10/10/2011

Lab #2 - Assessment Worksheet
IEEE 802.3 CSMA/CD & Ethernet II Networking

Course Name & Number: _____

Student Name: _____

Instructor Name: _____

Lab Due Date: _____

Overview

In this lab, students will learn to distinguish protocols which use the IEEE 802.3 and Ethernet II frames. Using the Wireshark Protocol Analyzer students will be able to filter, isolate and display IEEE 802.3 and Ethernet II within protocols captured and observe differences in frame formats, such as capacity, byte formatting and frame segmentation. Students will also be able to observe the various data transfer speeds of the different tiers of Ethernet in real-time. In addition they will be taught to understand and identify the differences in Hub/ Single and Switch/Multiple Broadcast Domains.

Lab Assessment Questions & Answers

1. Using the Wireshark Protocol Analyzer how were you able to isolate and inspect IP and CDP packets for further analysis?

2. In what section of the Wireshark Protocol Analyzer interface is the details of a captured packet frame displayed?

Current Version Date: 10/10/2011

3. Draw an IEEE 802.3 frame showing segments and bytes assigned for each segment?

4. What are the four main speeds of Ethernet?

5. What is the maximum size allocated for information in an IEEE 802.3 Ethernet frame?

6. What is the main difference in the layout of IEEE 802.3 and the Ethernet II frame?

7. What is the maximum number of bytes assigned to the "Source address" segment of an IEEE 802.3 frame

8. What are the differences in the functions of IEEE 802.3 and Ethernet v2 concerning the Layers of the OSI Model?

Current Version Date: 10/10/2011

9. When retrieving the 5MB file from the TargetWindows01 VM did you notice a difference in file transfer time using 10Mbps as compared to 100Mbps?

10. What are the advantages of the implementation of Multiple Broadcast Domains?

Current Version Date: 10/10/2011

Laboratory #3

Lab 3: TCP/IP Networking Communication Protocols

Learning Objectives and Outcomes

Upon completing this lab, students will be able to:

- Load and run Wireshark as a protocol analyzer and capture device.

- Analyze TCP/IP protocols using the Wireshark Protocol Analyzer.

- Identify Cisco proprietary and non-proprietary protocols.

- Perform and run network traffic statistics and analysis using Wireshark.

- Capture and decode common network protocols such as: ARP, DHCP, DNS and CDP

Required Setup and Tools

This course requires the use of the Onsite "Mock" IT Infrastructure and virtualized server farm. This is shown below:

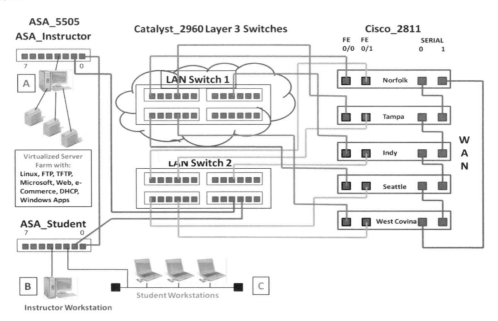

Figure 1 – Standard Onsite "Mock" IT Infrastructure & Virtualized Server Farm

The "Mock" IT Infrastructure is a preconfigured, IP network infrastructure complete with a classroom virtualized server farm. All IP addressing schema, VLAN configurations, and layer 3 switching is

Current Version Date: 10/10/2011

preconfigured. The IP networking infrastructure remains static and includes the following removable parts as indicated in Figure 1 above:

A) **NEEDED** – A classroom workstation (with at least 4 Gig RAM) capable of supporting an insert-able hard drive or USB hard drive with a preconfigured, virtualized server farm. This classroom workstation will support the virtualized VM server farm connected to the ASA_Instructor VLAN.

B) **NEEDED** – An "Instructor VM" workstation (with at least 2 Gig RAM) that shall act as the demonstration traffic generator for the protocol capture of equipment-based labs. The Instructor will engage ARP, DHCP, ICMP, TCP 3-way handshake, FTP, HTTP, TELNET, and SSH to demonstrate protocol interaction from a preconfigured Instructor Virtual Machine (VM). The Instructor workstation/server connects to the "ASA_Student" on any of the available ports to mimic the Student's configuration. These available ports are configured to be on the same logical VLAN; hence, any port can be used. The student lab workstations connect to the same "ASA_Student" on any of the available ports.

C) **NEEDED** – Student VM workstations (with at least 2 Gig RAM) use a preconfigured "Student VM" to act as an Attacker VM as well as a traffic monitoring and protocol capture device. Since all the ports on the "ASA_Student" are on the same VLAN, student workstations must connect to any of the ports on the ASA5505. Students must capture the protocol interaction by generating their own unique attack traffic to their target VM in order to answer Lab #3 - Assessment Worksheet questions.

The following summarizes the setup, configuration, and equipment needed to perform Lab #3:

- Standard Onsite "Mock" IT Infrastructure configuration and setup
  - Cisco 28xx routers, 29xx catalyst LAN switches, and ASA 5505 firewalls
  - TELNET accessible Cisco routers, SSH accessible Cisco routers, ICMP enabled on Cisco routers
- A virtualized server farm with:
  - A Microsoft Server VM for DHCP and other required network services
  - A Student and/or "Instructor VM" to use as the "Attacker VM" and traffic monitor
  - A "Target VM" Microsoft and/or Linux Server with the following:
    - Sample Website supporting HTTP and/or HTTPS
  - FTP and TFTP services enabled

- TCP/IP protocol primer cheat sheet with well-known port numbers (Included at the end of the lab manual.)

- Standard onsite Instructor and "Student VM" must have the following software applications loaded to perform this lab:

    - VMWare Player

- Standard Instructor and "Student VM" will be preconfigured with the following software:

    - Wireshark 1.2.9 for packet capturing and protocol analysis

    - TELNET and SSH open source client software – PuTTY

    - FTP and TFTP open source client software – FileZilla and TFTPd32

    - Adobe Reader for PDF Documentation

    - Microsoft Word for Lab Assessment Worksheet Questions & Answer

Equipment-Based Lab #3 – Student Steps:

Students should perform the following steps:

1. Insert your student removable hard drive or USB hard drive into a classroom workstation with VMWare Player pre-loaded

2. Boot up the "Student VM" workstation ("Student VM")

3. Boot up the Student Target VM workstation ("Target VM")

4. Log into your Student VM

5. Start the Wireshark application on the "Student VM" and click "Start Capture"

6. Engage the command prompt on the "Student VM" and PING various IP hosts, Cisco router interfaces, and LAN switch ports on this IP subnetwork: (Zenmap Gui scan of 172.30.0.0/24)

7. Run the PuTTY application from the "Student VM" and enter the targeted IP address of LAN Switch 1 and LAN Switch 2

8. TELNET to LAN Switch 1 172.16.8.5 and enter the Terminal console password "cisco"

9. SSH to LAN Switch 2 172.16.20.5 and enter the Terminal console password "cisco"

10. Start the FileZilla client application on the Student VM

11. FTP a file to the targeted FTP server: Dynamic IP Assigned to your Target VM, Port 21

    FTP Login information:

    Username: student

    Password : <blank>

Current Version Date: 10/10/2011

12. Start the Tftpd32 client application on the Student VM

13. TFTP a file to the targeted TFTP server: 172.30.0.52 port 67 or 69

14. "Stop Capture" in the Wireshark application.

15. Click in the "Filter" window in the Wireshark interface and type in "TCP" and hit "ENTER" to filter all TCP/IP packets. Identify and analyze the characteristics of the protocol displayed.

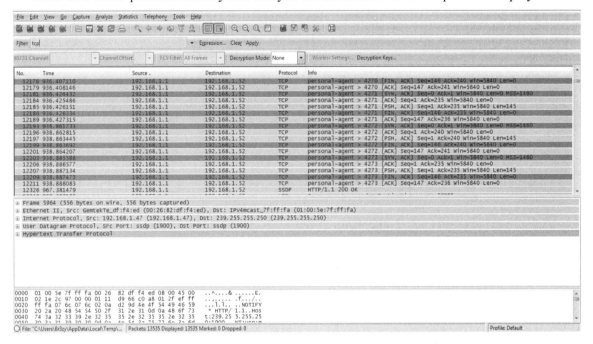

Figure 12 - Placing the Protocol into the Filter Window

16. Remove "TCP" from the filter window and redo the Step #15 inserting and using each of the following ARP, CDP, DNS and DHCP.

17. Clear the "Filter" window from the Wireshark interface to display all packets.

18. Navigate to the "Statistics" tab on the Wireshark interface and select "Summary". This shows the network statistics of the captured session.

Current Version Date: 10/10/2011

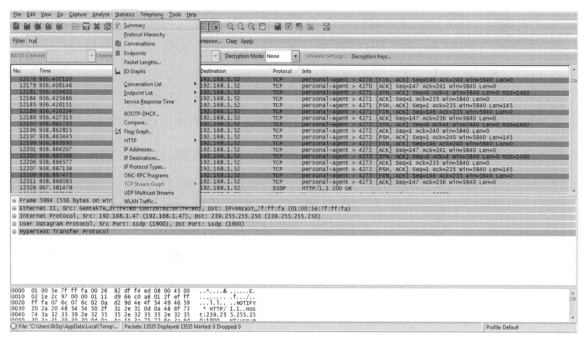

Figure 13 - Navigating to the Network Statistics Summary Tab

19. Create a screenshot of the "Summary window" of the network statistics and save it as "*YourName*

Lab#3 Summary"

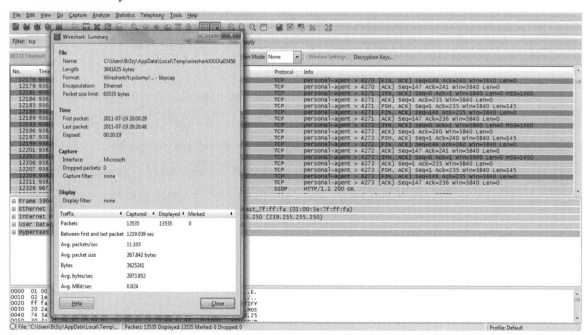

Figure 14 - Example of the Summary Window

Current Version Date: 10/10/2011

20. Save a screenshot of the Statistics analysis and name it "*YourName* Lab#3 Summary."

21. Save the Wireshark session as "*YourName* Lab#3 Capture.pcap"

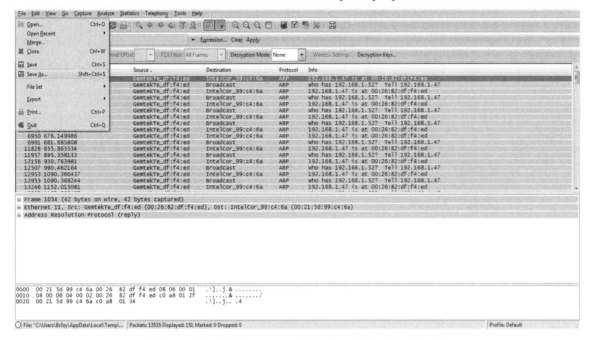

Figure 15 - Saving your Wireshark Session Capture

22. Send a softcopy of your "*YourName* Lab#3 Capture.pcap" file, requested screenshots for filtered protocol analysis, along with your completed Lab #3 Assessment Worksheet to your instructor.

Current Version Date: 10/10/2011

Student Lab Manual

Lab #3 – Supplement Sheet
TCP/IP Protocol Primer & Well-Known Port Numbers

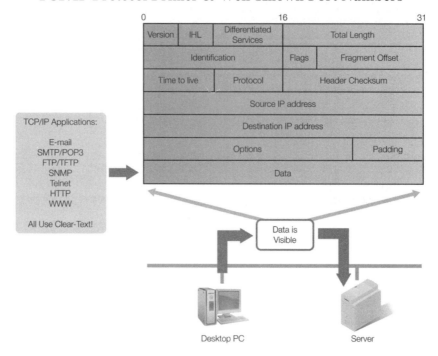

TCP/IP Figure 2 – IP Packet Header & Data Payload Field

FTP	File Transfer Protocol	Port #21
SSH	Secure Shell	Port #22
TELNET	Tele-Network	Port #23
SMTP	Simple Mail Transfer Protocol	Port #25
WHOIS	WHO IS	Port #43
DNS	Domain Name Service	Port #53
DHCP	Dynamic Host Control Protocol	Port #67
TFTP	Trivial File Transfer Protocol	Port #69
HTTP	Hyper Text Transfer Protocol	Port #80
POP3	Post Office Protocol 3	Port #110
SFTP	Secure File Transfer Protocol	Port #115
SNMP	Simple Network Management Protocol	Port #161
HTTPS	Hyper Text Transfer Protocol Secure	Port #443

Current Version Date: 10/10/2011

Deliverables

Upon completion of the TCP/IP Networking Communication Protocols Lab, students are required to provide the following deliverables:

1. Screenshots of filtered Capture statistics for each of the protocols (TCP, ARP, DNS, DHCP and CDP),

2. Screenshot of the Network Statistics Summary.

3. Soft copy of the Wireshark session capture file named "*YourName* Lab#3 Capture.pcap".

4. Lab #3 - Assessment Worksheet with answers to the assessment questions.

Evaluation Criteria and Rubrics

The following are the evaluation criteria and rubrics for Lab #3 that the students must perform:

1. Was the student able to load and run Wireshark as a protocol analyzer and capture device?- **[20%]**

2. Was the student able to analyze TCP/IP protocols using Wireshark as a protocol analyzer? - **[20%]**

3. Was the student able to identify Cisco proprietary and non-proprietary protocols? - **[20%]**

4. Was the student able to perform and run network traffic statistics and analysis using Wireshark? - **[20%]**

5. Was the student able to capture and decode common network protocols such as: ARP, DHCP, DNS and CDP? - **[20%]**

Lab #3 - Assessment Worksheet

TCP\IP Networking Communication Protocols

Course Name & Number: _____

Student Name: _____

Instructor Name: _____

Lab Due Date: _____

Overview

One of the most important tools needed for information systems security practitioners is a packet capture and protocol analysis tool. Wireshark is a freeware tool providing basic packet capture and protocol decoding capabilities. In this lab, students will become familiar with identifying and decoding common networking protocols such as ARP, DHCP, DNS, CDP and TCP/IP using Wireshark. In addition students will learn how to source required information from a Wireshark capture in order to perform and run network traffic statistics and analysis.

Lab Assessment Questions & Answers

1. What is the purpose of the address resolution protocol (ARP)?

2. What is the purpose of the dynamic host control protocol (DHCP)?

3. What is the purpose of the dynamic name service protocol (DNS)?

Current Version Date: 10/10/2011

4. List any two (2) other protocols observed within the Wireshark capture and their purposes?

5. What was the DHCP allocated source IP host address for the "Student VM" and Target VM?

6. Did the targeted IP host respond to the ICMP echo-request packet with an ICMP echo-reply packet? If yes, how many ICMP echo-request packets were sent back to the IP source?

7. Find a TCP 3-way handshake for a TELNET session. What is the significance of the TCP 3-way handshake?

8. What is the purpose of the Cisco discovery protocol (CDP)?

9. Why is using TELNET a security risk for an IP network infrastructure?

10. What details of network statistics is displayed in the Wireshark interface's Summary Display section?

Current Version Date: 10/10/2011

Laboratory #4

Lab 4: Designing an IP Addressing Schema for Networking Infrastructure

Learning Objectives and Outcomes

Upon completing this lab, students will be able to:

- Review the current IPv4 and IPv6 addressing scheme/structure.

- Align Subnet masks to corresponding number of IP sub-networks and IP hosts.

- Identify requirements for designing an IP addressing schema.

- Design an IPv4 addressing schema for Layer 2 and Layer 3 Networking.

- Design an IPv6 addressing schema for Layer 2 and Layer 3 Networking.

Required Setup and Tools

This course requires the use of the Onsite "Mock" IT Infrastructure and virtualized server farm. This is shown below:

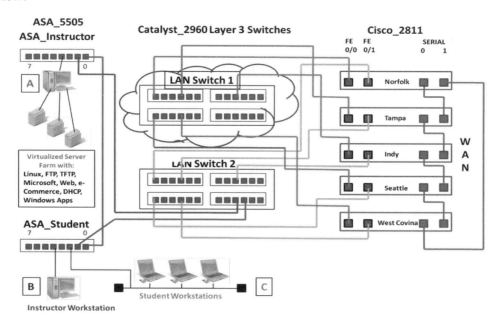

Figure 1 – Standard Onsite "Mock" IT Infrastructure & Virtualized Server Farm

The "Mock" IT Infrastructure is a preconfigured, IP network infrastructure complete with a classroom virtualized server farm. All IP addressing schema, VLAN configurations, and layer 3 switching is

Current Version Date: 10/10/2011

preconfigured. The IP networking infrastructure remains static and includes the following removable parts as indicated in Figure 1 above:

A) **NEEDED** – A classroom workstation (with at least 4 Gig RAM) capable of supporting an insert-able hard drive or USB hard drive with a preconfigured, virtualized server farm. This classroom workstation will support the virtualized VM server farm connected to the ASA_Instructor VLAN.

B) **NEEDED** – An "Instructor VM" workstation (with at least 2 Gig RAM) that shall act as the demonstration traffic generator for the protocol capture of equipment-based labs. The Instructor will engage ARP, DHCP, ICMP, TCP 3-way handshake, FTP, HTTP, TELNET, and SSH to demonstrate protocol interaction from a preconfigured Instructor Virtual Machine (VM). The Instructor workstation/server connects to the "ASA_Student" on any of the available ports to mimic the Student's configuration. These available ports are configured to be on the same logical VLAN; hence, any port can be used. The student lab workstations connect to the same "ASA_Student" on any of the available ports.

C) **NEEDED** – "Student VM" workstations (with at least 2 Gig RAM) use a preconfigured "Student VM" to act as an Attacker VM as well as a traffic monitoring and protocol capture device. Since all the ports on the "ASA_Student" are on the same VLAN, student workstations must connect to any of the ports on the ASA5505. Students must capture the protocol interaction by generating their own unique attack traffic to their target VM in order to answer Lab #4 - Assessment Worksheet questions.

The following summarizes the setup, configuration, and equipment needed to perform Lab #4:

- Standard Onsite "Mock" IT Infrastructure configuration and setup
    - Cisco 28xx routers, 29xx catalyst LAN switches, and ASA 5505 firewalls
    - TELNET accessible Cisco routers, SSH accessible Cisco routers, ICMP enabled on Cisco routers
- A virtualized server farm with:
    - A Microsoft Server VM for DHCP and other required network services
    - A Student and/or "Instructor VM" to use as the "Attacker VM" and traffic monitor
    - A "Target VM" Microsoft and/or Linux Server with the following:
        - Sample Website supporting HTTP and/or HTTPS
    - FTP and TFTP services enabled

Current Version Date: 10/10/2011

- TCP/IP protocol primer cheat sheet with well-known port numbers (Included at the end of the lab manual.)

- Standard onsite Instructor and "Student VM" must have the following software applications loaded to perform this lab:
    - VMWare Player

- Standard Instructor and "Student VM" will be preconfigured with the following software:
    - Wireshark 1.2.9 for packet capturing and protocol analysis
    - TELNET and SSH open source client software – PuTTY
    - FTP and TFTP open source client software – FileZilla and TFTPd32
    - Zenamp GUI / NMAP port scanning tool.
    - Adobe Reader for PDF Documentation
    - Microsoft Word for Lab Assessment Worksheet Questions & Answer

Equipment-Based Lab #4 – Student Steps:

Students should perform the following steps:

1. Insert your Student removable hard drive or USB hard drive to a classroom workstation

2. Start the VMWare Player application on the classroom workstation

3. Boot up and log into your Student VM

4. Retrieve the following reconnaissance information:
    - Source IP host addresses for the ASA Student
    - Source IP host addresses for LAN Switch 1

5. Start the Zenmap GUI /Nmap application initiate a ping sweep of the network.

6. Zenmap Gui scan of 172.30.0.0/24 and select "ping scan" from the drop down box in the scan profile window.

Current Version Date: 10/10/2011

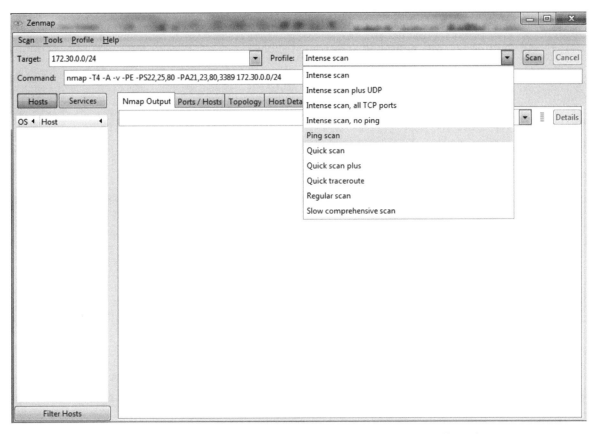

Figure 16 - Selecting the Ping Scan Profile on the Nmap Interface

7. Once the scan is completed navigate and click on the network topology tab to access the graphical layout of the network. Save the graphic as "*YourName* Lab#4 Graphic".

8. From the "Student VM" load the PuTTY application and TELNET to LAN Switch 1 and LAN Switch 2 to perform the network documentation task.

    LAN Switch 1 target IP address: 172.16.8.5

    LAN Switch 2 target IP address: 172.16.20.5

9. Once connected remotely access Cisco 28xx routers and the Cisco ASA Instructor using the same terminal console password configured on LAN Switch 1 and LAN Switch 2 to retrieve further IP address information.

10. Using the information gathered provide and list the following network documentation and insert into the Lab#4 Network Documentation Table.

    *   **IP host addresses and version type (IPv4 or IPv6)** for all ports that are enabled within the Cisco IP networking infrastructure.

    *   **IP subnet mask address** for the IP environment

    *   **IP sub network slash notation** for corresponding subnets.

Current Version Date: 10/10/2011

- **Total number of IP hosts** that are found on the ASA Student VLAN
- **IP default gateway router** IP address and subnet mask address for the Cisco IP networking infrastructure.

Deliverables

Upon completion of Designing an IP Addressing Schema for Networking Infrastructure Lab, students are required to provide the following deliverables:

1. A softcopy of the Zenmap/Nmap network topology graphic labeled *"YourName* Lab#4 Graphic".
2. A completed version of the Lab #4 Network Documentation Table.
3. A Word Document entailing the IPv4 and IPv6 addressing solutions for the Lab #4 Scenario.
4. Lab #4 - Assessment Worksheet with answers to the assessment questions.

Evaluation Criteria and Rubrics

The following are the evaluation criteria and rubrics for Lab #4 that the students must perform:

1. Was the student able to review the current IPv4 and IPv6 addressing scheme/structure? - **[20%]**
2. Was the student able to align Subnet masks to corresponding number of IP sub-networks and IP hosts? - **[20%]**
3. Was the student able to identify requirements for designing an IP addressing schema? - **[20%]**
4. Was the student able to design an IPv4 addressing schema for Layer 2 and Layer 3 Networking? - **[20%]**
5. Was the student able to design an IPv6 addressing schema for Layer 2 and Layer 3 Networking? - **[20%]**

Lab #4 Scenario

Designing an IPv4 and IPv6 Network Addressing Schema
for The Marketing Company Inc.

The management of The Marketing Company Inc. has decided to redesign their internal network for the Marketing and Sales departments. Contracting the services of Network Evolutions Inc., they have submitted the following requirements:

- Build and IPv4 addressing schema for the Sales and Marketing departments
- The IP addressing schema must be "Class C"
- The Marketing and Sales Departments both hold 125 workstations each
- The Marketing and Sales Department must be on different subnets respectively

As a Network Engineer for Network Evolutions Inc., you must configure LAN Switch 2 to provide the requirements for the management of The Marketing Company Inc. Marketing and Sales departments and list the following:

1. **Class C IP Address**
2. **The host IP address ranges for Marketing and Sales**
3. **The number of total IP addresses each subnet can facilitate**
4. **The Subnet mask**
5. **The Subnet ID**
6. **Maximum amount of Subnets**
7. **The Broadcast Address**

The management of The Marketing Company Inc. also requires you to design an IPv6 addressing schema based on the same Ipv4 configuration. For the IPv6 schema provide the following information:

1. **IP address**
2. **The Subnet mask**
3. **Maximum number of Subnets**
4. **Maximum number of Hosts**

Complete the answers on a Word Document, Times New Roman font size 12, regular spacing and submit.

Note: Refer to the Lab #4 IP Schema Network Design Diagram sheet for visual reference. You can also use the link to the online subnetting calculator to assist in building your schema http://www.subnet-calculator.com/subnet.php?net_class=C and the IPv4 to IPv6 Calculator http://www.subnetonline.com/pages/subnet-calculators/ipv4-to-ipv6-converter.php

Lab #4 - Worksheet

Network Documentation Table

Host Device	IP Address on Ports	Default Gateway	Subnet Mask	Slash Notation
ASA_Student				
ASA_Instructor				
LAN Switch 1				
LAN Switch 2				
Norfolk				
Indy				
Tampa				
Seattle				
West Covina				

The total number of IP hosts that are found on the ASA Student's VLAN is? : _____

Current Version Date: 10/10/2011

Lab #4 IP Schema Network Design Diagram

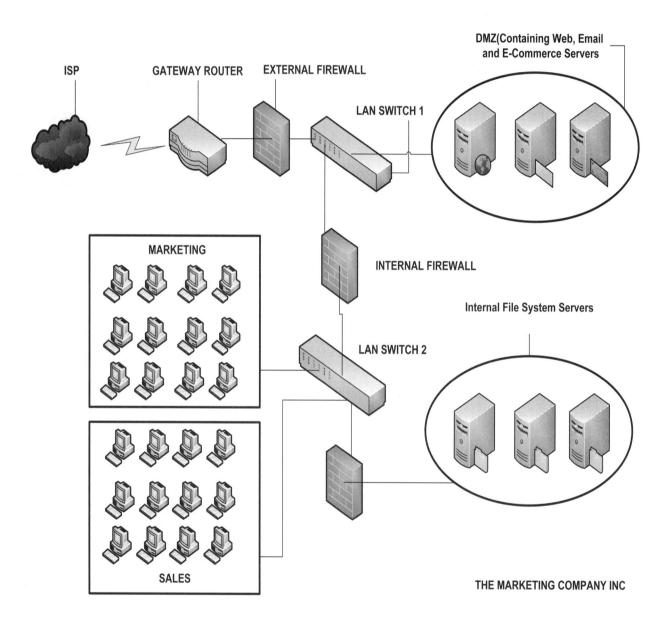

Current Version Date: 10/10/2011

Lab #4 – Supplement Sheet
IP Subnet Masks

IP-Subnet-Mask numbers

IP mask numbers are used to divide internet addresses into blocks called subnets. The mask number represents the number of 1s in the binary of the address that is "masked" against the address so that it ignores the last bits which are for the group of IP addresses in the masked address.

The first address of a subnet block (all 0s) is called the network address or network ID. The last address (all 1s) is the broadcast address of the network. Typically the network address +1 or the broadcast address -1 is the gateway to the internet. The 'slash' notation (ie /24) is known as CIDR format, while the more conventional 255.255.255.0 notation is considered a subnet mask.

Net Bits	Subnet Mask	Total-Addresses
/20	255.255.240.0	4096
/21	255.255.248.0	2048
/22	255.255.252.0	1024
/23	255.255.254.0	512
/24	255.255.255.0	256
/25	255.255.255.128	128
/26	255.255.255.192	64
/27	255.255.255.224	32
/28	255.255.255.240	16
/29	255.255.255.248	8
/30	255.255.255.252	4

The first address of a subnet block (all 0s) is called the network address or network ID. The last address (all 1s) is the broadcast address of the network. Typically the network address +1 or the broadcast address -1 is the gateway to the internet. This leaves us with total number of IP numbers -3 left over for host address with in a sub net block. That is why you either get 1 IP (4-3= 1) or if you ask for one more you get 5 (8-3=5).

Current Version Date: 10/10/2011

Here is an example:

192.168.1.0/25 would include all address between 192.168.1.0 and 192.168.1.127

while 192.168.1.128/25 would include 192.168.1.128 and 192.168.1.255

Below is a mask table that makes it easy to look up the mask for a group of IP addresses.

Mask Table

255.255.240.0

Mask = /24

255.255.240.0 0-255

Mask = /25

  0-127
  128-255

Mask = /26

  0-63
  64-127
  128-191
  192-255

Mask = /27

  0-31
  32-63
  64-95
  96-127
  128-159
  160-191
  192-223
  224-255

Mask = /28

  0-15
  16-31
  32-47
  48-63
  64-79
  80-95
  96-111
  112-127
  128-143
  144-159
  160-175
  176-191

Current Version Date: 10/10/2011

192-207
208-223
224-239
240-255

Mask = /29

 0-7
8-15
16-23
24-31
32-39
40-47
48-55
56-63
64-71
72-79
80-87
88-95
96-103
104-111
112-119
120-127
128-135
136-143
144-151
152-159
160-167
168-175
176-183
184-191
192-199
200-207
208-215
216-223
224-231
232-239
240-247
248-255

Mask = /30

0-3
4-7
8-11
12-15
16-19
20-23
24-27
28-31

Current Version Date: 10/10/2011

32-35
36-39
40-43
44-47
48-51
52-55
56-59
60-63
64-67
68-71
72-75
76-79
80-83
84-87
88-91
92-95
96-99
100-103
104-107
108-111
112-115
116-119
120-123
124-127
128-131
132-135
136-139
140-143
144-147
148-151
152-155
156-159
160-163
164-167
168-171
172-175
176-179
180-183
184-187
188-191
192-195
196-199
200-203
204-207
208-211
212-215

Current Version Date: 10/10/2011

216-219
220-223
224-227
228-231
232-235
236-239
240-243
244-247
248-251
252-255

Current Version Date: 10/10/2011

Netmasks

Netmask	Netmask (binary)	CIDR	Notes
255.255.255.255	11111111.11111111.11111111.11111111	/32	Host (single addr)
255.255.255.254	11111111.11111111.11111111.11111110	/31	Unusable
255.255.255.252	11111111.11111111.11111111.11111100	/30	2 usable
255.255.255.248	11111111.11111111.11111111.11111000	/29	6 usable
255.255.255.240	11111111.11111111.11111111.11110000	/28	14 usable
255.255.255.224	11111111.11111111.11111111.11100000	/27	30 usable
255.255.255.192	11111111.11111111.11111111.11000000	/26	62 usable
255.255.255.128	11111111.11111111.11111111.10000000	/25	126 usable
255.255.255.0	11111111.11111111.11111111.00000000	/24	"Class C" 254 usable
255.255.254.0	11111111.11111111.11111110.00000000	/23	2 Class C's
255.255.252.0	11111111.11111111.11111100.00000000	/22	4 Class C's
255.255.248.0	11111111.11111111.11111000.00000000	/21	8 Class C's
255.255.240.0	11111111.11111111.11110000.00000000	/20	16 Class C's
255.255.224.0	11111111.11111111.11100000.00000000	/19	32 Class C's
255.255.192.0	11111111.11111111.11000000.00000000	/18	64 Class C's
255.255.128.0	11111111.11111111.10000000.00000000	/17	128 Class C's
255.255.0.0	11111111.11111111.00000000.00000000	/16	"Class B"
255.254.0.0	11111111.11111110.00000000.00000000	/15	2 Class B's
255.252.0.0	11111111.11111100.00000000.00000000	/14	4 Class B's
255.248.0.0	11111111.11111000.00000000.00000000	/13	8 Class B's
255.240.0.0	11111111.11110000.00000000.00000000	/12	16 Class B's
255.224.0.0	11111111.11100000.00000000.00000000	/11	32 Class B's
255.192.0.0	11111111.11000000.00000000.00000000	/10	64 Class B's
255.128.0.0	11111111.10000000.00000000.00000000	/9	128 Class B's
255.0.0.0	11111111.00000000.00000000.00000000	/8	"Class A"
254.0.0.0	11111110.00000000.00000000.00000000	/7	
252.0.0.0	11111100.00000000.00000000.00000000	/6	
248.0.0.0	11111000.00000000.00000000.00000000	/5	
240.0.0.0	11110000.00000000.00000000.00000000	/4	"Class E" (Multicast and reserved)
224.0.0.0	11100000.00000000.00000000.00000000	/3	
192.0.0.0	11000000.00000000.00000000.00000000	/2	
128.0.0.0	10000000.00000000.00000000.00000000	/1	
0.0.0.0	00000000.00000000.00000000.00000000	/0	IP space

Current Version Date: 10/10/2011

Lab #4 – Assessment Worksheet

Designing an IP Addressing Schema for Networking Infrastructure

Course Name & Number: _____

Student Name: _____

Instructor Name: _____

Lab Due Date: _____

Overview

In this lab, students will learn how to determine the IPv4 /IPv6 network design, implementation and topology by performing a network discovery scan using Zenamp GUI (Nmap). After performing the initial IP network discovery task, identifying the type of IP version, range and subnetting scheme used they will then perform IP network documentation of the Mock IT infrastructure. In addition students will learn how to determine the requirements to design their own IPv4 and IPv6 addressing scheme to facilitate the needs of an organization using online tools such as IPv4/IPv6 subnet calculators and referring to IP addressing schema design best practices.

Lab Assessment Questions & Answers

1. What are the three types of IPv4 classes and what are the maximum amount of addresses they can facilitate respectively?

Current Version Date: 10/10/2011

2. What are the private address ranges of each of the three IPv4 classes

3. How many bits does IPv4 use in comparison to IPv6 ?

4. What is the major advantage that IPv6 has over IPv4 concerning the number of available addresses it can supply and security?

5. What information is necessary when judging the scalability of building an IPv4 or IPv6 schema for a network?

6. What is the subnet mask that corresponds to the slash notation "/32"?

Current Version Date: 10/10/2011

7. Name three (3) other scans that are listed in the scan "profile" section of the Zenmap(Nmap) Gui interface.

8. What information does the "Topology" tab display in the Zenmap GUI (Nmap) application after a scan is completed?

9. What is the IP subnet number for the server farm VLAN where the classroom workstation with virtualized server farm is located (ASA_Instructor VLAN)?

10. What is the Zenmap GUI (Nmap) ping scan used for?

Current Version Date: 10/10/2011

Laboratory #5

Lab 5: IEEE 802.11a/b/g/h/i/n Wireless LAN

Learning Objectives and Outcomes

Upon completing this lab, students will be able to:

- Align the steps needed to design a WLAN infrastructure.

- Identify vulnerable key points within the WLAN infrastructure.

- Secure a Wireless LAN.

- Disable SSID broadcasting on a Wireless LAN.

- Create a WLAN implementation plan.

Required Setup and Tools

This course requires the use of the Onsite "Mock" IT Infrastructure and virtualized server farm. This is shown below:

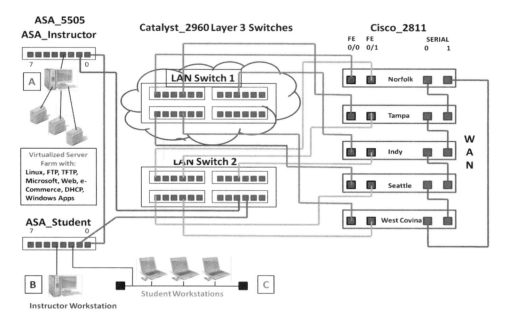

Figure 1 – Standard Onsite "Mock" IT Infrastructure & Virtualized Server Farm

The "Mock" IT Infrastructure is a preconfigured, IP network infrastructure complete with a classroom virtualized server farm. All IP addressing schema, VLAN configurations, and layer 3 switching is

Current Version Date: 10/10/2011

preconfigured. The IP networking infrastructure remains static and includes the following removable parts as indicated in Figure 1 above:

A) **NEEDED** – A classroom workstation (with at least 4 Gig RAM) capable of supporting an insert-able hard drive or USB hard drive with a preconfigured, virtualized server farm. This classroom workstation will support the virtualized VM server farm connected to the ASA_Instructor VLAN.

B) **NEEDED** – An instructor VM workstation (with at least 2 Gig RAM) that shall act as the demonstration traffic generator for the protocol capture of equipment-based labs. The Instructor will engage ARP, DHCP, ICMP, TCP 3-way handshake, FTP, HTTP, TELNET, and SSH to demonstrate protocol interaction from a preconfigured Instructor Virtual Machine (VM). The Instructor workstation/server connects to the "ASA_Student" on any of the available ports to mimic the Student's configuration. These available ports are configured to be on the same logical VLAN; hence, any port can be used. The student lab workstations connect to the same "ASA_Student" on any of the available ports.

C) **NEEDED** – Student VM workstations (with at least 2 Gig RAM) use a preconfigured Student VM to act as an Attacker VM as well as a traffic monitoring and protocol capture device. Since all the ports on the "ASA_Student" are on the same VLAN, student workstations must connect to any of the ports on the ASA5505. Students must capture the protocol interaction by generating their own unique attack traffic to their target VM in order to answer Lab #5 - Assessment Worksheet questions.

The following summarizes the setup, configuration, and equipment needed to perform Lab #5:

- Standard Onsite "Mock" IT Infrastructure configuration and setup
    - Cisco 28xx routers, 29xx catalyst LAN switches, and ASA 5505 firewalls
    - TELNET accessible Cisco routers, SSH accessible Cisco routers, ICMP enabled on Cisco routers
- A virtualized server farm with:
    - A Microsoft Server VM for DHCP and other required network services
    - A Student and/or Instructor VM to use as the "Attacker VM" and traffic monitor
    - A "Target VM" Microsoft and/or Linux Server with the following:
        - Sample Website supporting HTTP and/or HTTPS
    - FTP and TFTP services enabled

Current Version Date: 10/10/2011

- TCP/IP protocol primer cheat sheet with well-known port numbers (Included at the end of the lab manual.)

- Standard onsite Instructor and Student VM must have the following software applications loaded to perform this lab:

  - VMWare Player

- Standard Instructor and Student VM will be preconfigured with the following software:

  - An internet browser such as Internet Explorer, Mozilla Firefox etc.

  - Microsoft Word for construction and completion of Lab #5 Scenarios and Lab Assessment Worksheet Questions & Answers.

Equipment-Based Lab #5 – Student Steps:

Students should perform the following steps:

1. Insert your Student removable hard drive or USB hard drive to a classroom workstation

2. Start the VMWare Player application on the classroom workstation

3. Boot up and log into your Student VM.

4. The following e-reference articles will provide students with the following:

   - Information on IEEE 802.11 a/b/g/h/i and n standards specifically.

   - Assist students in learning the key steps for determining the requirements for designing a WLAN infrastructure.

5. Using the Internet Explorer or Mozilla Firefox Browser, navigate to the following reference material:

   - Refer to The IEEE Standards Association Site for IEEE 802.11 a/b/g/h/i and n standards - http://standards.ieee.org/about/get/802/802.11.html

   - Refer to the **"Wireless Design Guide"** Lab handout for key steps in determining requirements for designing a WLAN Infrastructure.

   - Refer to **"SANS Security Guidelines for WLAN Implementation"** Lab handout for recommendations and best practices for securing WLAN infrastructure.

6. Using the gathered information in Step 5, complete the Lab #5 Scenario I - Aligning the Required Steps for Designing a WLAN Infrastructure, located at the end of this lab.

7. To identify vulnerable key points within a WLAN infrastructure refer to the SANS Security Vulnerabilities & Wireless LAN Technology Lab handout and complete the Lab #5 Identifying Key Vulnerabilities in WLAN Infrastructure table below.

8. To secure a Wireless Network using WPA2 encryption, disabling SSID broadcasting and other Wireless Security options - Refer to the "Lab #5 WiFi Security Tutorial" demo video.

9. Move on Lab #5 Scenario II - Designing a WLAN Implementation Plan for the School of Information Technology providing Scenario I is completed.

Deliverables

Upon completion of IEEE 802.11a/b/g/h/i/n Wireless LAN Lab, students are required to provide the following deliverables:

1. A Microsoft Word document containing the pre-implementation report for Lab #5 Scenario I, Aligning the Steps for Designing & Implementing WLAN Infrastructure.

2. A Microsoft Word document containing a detailed WLAN Implementation plan for Lab #5 Scenario II, Designing a WLAN Implementation Plan for The School of Information Technology.

Evaluation Criteria and Rubrics

The following are the evaluation criteria and rubrics for Lab #5 that the students must perform:

1. Was the student able to successfully align the steps needed to design a WLAN infrastructure? - **[20%]**

2. Was the student able to successfully identify vulnerable key points within the WLAN infrastructure? - **[20%]**

3. Was the student able to secure a Wireless LAN? - **[20%]**

4. Was the student able to successfully disable SSID broadcasting on a Wireless LAN? - **[20%]**

5. Was the student able to successfully create a WLAN implementation plan? - **[20%]**

Current Version Date: 10/10/2011

Lab #5 Scenario I

Aligning the Required Steps for Designing & Implementing a WLAN Infrastructure

The Management of the School of Information Technology has contracted the services of Network Evolutions Inc. to provide a requirement list for implementation of WLAN infrastructure into their current network. The implementation of WLAN into the current network will provide students with secure wireless access to the campus' internal network in addition to internet access via their laptops, multimedia tablets, smartphones etc.

The School of Information Technology has never had WLAN preparation procedures performed on the campus site. As Network Evolutions Inc. lead WLAN Consultant you are required to formulate a report consisting of the necessary requirements taken into consideration for WLAN implementation. Key points to consider for your report:

- **What procedures should be performed on site prior to implementation?**
- **Who/What type of users will most utilize WLAN resources?**
- **What applications do users and administration intend to use?**
- **What types of devices will be used to access the network?**
- **What areas on campus will need wireless coverage?**
- **What type of information will be sent across the WLAN?**

Students are required to construct their report on a Word Document, Times New Roman font size 12, regular spacing and submit to the instructor.

** Note: Refer students to the **"Wireless Design Guide"** and **"SANS Security Guidelines for WLAN Implementation"** Lab handouts to which can be used as a guideline to build their report.

Current Version Date: 10/10/2011

Lab #5

Identifying Key Vulnerabilities in WLAN Infrastructure

No.	VULNERABILITY	DESCRIPTION	ASSESSED RISK	METHOD OF REMEDIATION
1	No configured/Poor security			
2	No set physical boundaries			
3	Physically insecure locations			
4	Rogue access points			
5	Unsecured holes in the Network			

Note: Refer to the "**SANS Security Vulnerabilities & Wireless LAN Technology**" lab handout for information related for completing the above table.

Current Version Date: 10/10/2011

Lab #5 Scenario II

Designing a WLAN Implementation Plan for The School Of Information Technology

The management of the School of Information Technology has reviewed and approved Network Evolutions Inc.'s WLAN requirements report and is ready to continue onto the implementation stage.

As Network Evolutions Inc. lead WLAN Consultant you are required to construct an Implementation Plan for seamless and secure wireless networking implementation. Key points necessary to consider for WLAN implementation are as follows:

- **RF Planning** - site survey for details coverage, capacity and performance of the WLAN
- **User Applications & Devices** - types of users, applications and devices that will be used on the WLAN infrastructure.
- **Security** - recommendations for secure access, wireless intrusion detection & prevention methods, monitoring etc.
- **System Management** - management of users, device access, applications etc
- **Scalability** - recommendations to facilitate plans for future network infrastructure growth.
- **Redundancy/Reliability** - recommendations for maintenance of network availability and resiliency.

Submit a detailed plan by identifying and determining all areas or implementation suitable for the campus. Construct your WLAN Implementation Plan on a Word Document, Times New Roman font size 12, regular spacing and submit to the instructor.

** Note: Use the information gathered for the Lab #5 Scenario I and use it as the foundation to construct the WLAN Implementation Plan. Refer to the **"Wireless Design Guide"** and **"SANS Security Guidelines for WLAN Implementation"** Lab handouts to which can be used as a guideline for formatting and building your plan.

Lab #5 - Assessment Worksheet
IEEE 802.11a/b/g/h/i/n Wireless LAN

Course Name & Number: _____

Student Name: _____

Instructor Name: _____

Lab Due Date: _____

Overview

In this lab, students will learn about IEEE 802.11 Wireless Networking aligning the steps needed to design and implement WLAN infrastructure. This lab utilizes the SANS Institute resource material as the largest source for information security training as a guide for students to expand their real world knowledge on identifying vulnerable key points within the WLAN infrastructure, securing a Wireless LAN. Using all the gathered practical and theoretic knowledge, students learn how to create their own structured WLAN Implementation Plan for real world scenarios.

Lab Assessment Questions & Answers

1. Define the term Wireless LAN?

2. What are three (3) advantages of implementing Wireless LAN?

Current Version Date: 10/10/2011

3. What are three disadvantages of implementing Wireless LAN?

4. What is the maximum data rate of IEEE 802.11 g?

5. Which version of the IEEE 802.11 Wireless standards is the fastest and why?

6. How do you gain access to the wireless router configuration to enable security settings?

7. What is the default username and password of the Netgear Router used in the tutorial video?

8. For security purposes, why should you change the default password for the Netgear Router?

Current Version Date: 10/10/2011

9. Define the term "SSID"?

10. What is meant by the term SSID Broadcasting?

11. Name three (3) key vulnerabilities in WLAN infrastructure and how they can be remediated?

12. What are three ways to secure a Wireless LAN?

13. What are the three (3) main security threats posed in the implementation of WLAN?

14. Define the term "RF Site Survey"?

15. What is the importance of performing and RF Survey prior to WLAN implementation?

Laboratory #6

Lab 6: IEEE Layer 2 Networking, Virtual LANs, and Resiliency

Learning Objectives and Outcomes

Upon completing this lab, students will be able to:

- Configure multiple Layer 2 Virtual LANs in a single Switch.

- Extend a Virtual LAN definition between two Switches.

- Configure Trunk links for the extended Virtual LAN

- Configure STP/RSTP for Layer 2 resiliency within the Mock IT Infrastructure

- Design a Layer 2 network solution for a collapsed building backbone.

Required Setup and Tools

This course requires the use of the Onsite "Mock" IT Infrastructure and virtualized server farm. This is shown below:

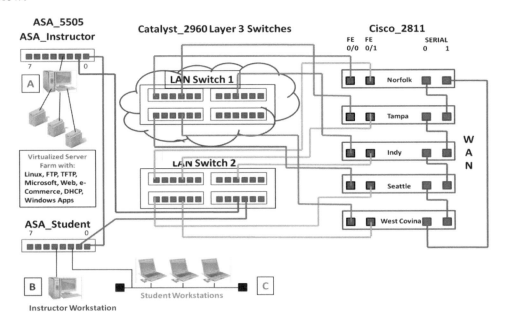

Figure 1 – Standard Onsite "Mock" IT Infrastructure & Virtualized Server Farm

Current Version Date: 10/10/2011

The "Mock" IT Infrastructure is a preconfigured, IP network infrastructure complete with a classroom virtualized server farm. All IP addressing schema, VLAN configurations, and layer 3 switching is preconfigured. The IP networking infrastructure remains static and includes the following removable parts as indicated in Figure 1 above:

A) **NEEDED** – A classroom workstation (with at least 4 Gig RAM) capable of supporting an insert-able hard drive or USB hard drive with a preconfigured, virtualized server farm. This classroom workstation will support the virtualized VM server farm connected to the ASA_Instructor VLAN.

B) **NEEDED** – An "Instructor VM" workstation (with at least 2 Gig RAM) that shall act as the demonstration traffic generator for the protocol capture of equipment-based labs. The Instructor will engage ARP, DHCP, ICMP, TCP 3-way handshake, FTP, HTTP, TELNET, and SSH to demonstrate protocol interaction from a preconfigured Instructor Virtual Machine (VM). The Instructor workstation/server connects to the "ASA_Student" on any of the available ports to mimic the Student's configuration. These available ports are configured to be on the same logical VLAN; hence, any port can be used. The student lab workstations connect to the same "ASA_Student" on any of the available ports.

C) **NEEDED** – "Student VM" workstations (with at least 2 Gig RAM) use a preconfigured "Student VM" to act as an Attacker VM as well as a traffic monitoring and protocol capture device. Since all the ports on the "ASA_Student" are on the same VLAN, student workstations must connect to any of the ports on the ASA5505. Students must capture the protocol interaction by generating their own unique attack traffic to their target VM in order to answer Lab #6 - Assessment Worksheet questions.

The following summarizes the setup, configuration, and equipment needed to perform Lab #6:

- Standard onsite "Mock" IT Infrastructure configuration and setup
  - Cisco 28xx routers, 29xx catalyst LAN switches, and ASA 5505 firewalls
  - TELNET accessible Cisco routers, SSH accessible Cisco routers, ICMP enabled on Cisco routers
- A virtualized server farm with:
  - A Microsoft Server VM for DHCP and other required network services
  - A Student and/or "Instructor VM" to use as the "Attacker VM" and traffic monitor
  - A "Target VM" Microsoft and/or Linux Server with the following:

- Sample Website supporting HTTP and/or HTTPS
    - FTP and TFTP services enabled
- TCP/IP protocol primer cheat sheet with well-known port numbers (Included at the end of the lab manual.)
- Standard onsite Instructor and "Student VM" must have the following software applications loaded to perform this lab:
    - VMWare Player
- Standard Instructor and "Student VM" will be preconfigured with the following software:
    - Wireshark 1.2.9 for packet capturing and protocol analysis
    - TELNET and SSH open source client software – PuTTY
    - FTP and TFTP open source client software – FileZilla and TFTPd32
    - Adobe Reader for PDF Documentation
    - Microsoft Word for Lab Assessment Worksheet Questions & Answer

Equipment-Based Lab #6 – Student Steps:

Students should perform the following steps:

1. Insert your Student removable hard drive or USB hard drive to a classroom workstation
2. Start the VMWare Player application on the classroom workstation
3. Boot up and log into your Student VM.
4. Follow the following sequence to create two new VLAN's ,VLAN0101 and VLAN0102 on LAN. SW1.
5. At the LAN.SW1 switch prompt enter the following:

   LAN.SW1>enable

   LAN.SW1#configure terminal

   Enter configuration commands, one per line. End with CNTL/Z.

   LAN.SW1(config)#vlan 0101

   LAN.SW1(config-vlan)#mtu 1500

   LAN.SW1(config-vlan)#end

   LAN.SW1#

   Mar 1 02:09:43.663: %SYS-5-CONFIG_I: Configured from console(LAN.SW1 displays configuration has changed)*

   LAN.SW1#configure terminal

Enter configuration commands, one per line. End with CNTL/Z.

LAN.SW1(config)#vlan 0102

LAN.SW1(config-vlan)#mtu 1500

LAN.SW1(config-vlan)#end

Mar 1 02:10:14.223: %SYS-5-CONFIG_I: Configured from console(LAN.SW1 displays configuration has changed)*

6. Use the "show vlan" command to verify that VLANs 0101 and 0102 has been created. Assign IP address to the VLANs, from the prompt enter the following:

LAN.SW1#configure terminal

Enter configuration commands, one per line. End with CNTL/Z.

LAN.SW1(config)#interface vlan0101

LAN.SW1(config-if)#ip address 192.168.1.1 255.255.255.0

LAN.SW1(config-if)#no shutdown

LAN.SW1(config-if)#end

LAN.SW1#

Mar 1 02:21:21.402: %SYS-5-CONFIG_I: Configured from console

LAN.SW1#configure terminal

Enter configuration commands, one per line. End with CNTL/Z.

LAN.SW1(config)#interface vlan0102

LAN.SW1(config-if)#ip address 192.168.2.1 255.255.255.0

LAN.SW1(config-if)#no shutdown

LAN.SW1(config-if)#end

LAN.SW1#

Mar 1 02:21:21.402: %SYS-5-CONFIG_I: Configured from console

7. Assign access ports for the VLANs. VLAN 0101 will be assigned Fastethernet ports 0/21 - 0/22 and VLAN 0102 will be assigned Fastethernet ports 0/23 - 0/24. At the prompt enter the following:

LAN.SW1#configure terminal

Enter configuration commands, one per line. End with CNTL/Z.

LAN.SW1(config)#interface range fa0/21 - 22

LAN.SW1(config-if-range)#switchport mode access

LAN.SW1(config-if-range)#switch access vlan 0101

LAN.SW1(config-if-range)#end

Current Version Date: 10/10/2011

LAN.SW1#

*Mar 1 02:39:15.781: %SYS-5-CONFIG_I: Configured from console by console

LAN.SW1#configure terminal

Enter configuration commands, one per line. End with CNTL/Z.

LAN.SW1(config)#interface range fa0/23 - 24

LAN.SW1(config-if-range)#switchport mode access

LAN.SW1(config-if-range)#switch access vlan 0102

LAN.SW1(config-if-range)#end

LAN.SW1#

*Mar 1 02:39:15.781: %SYS-5-CONFIG_I: Configured from console by console

8. Use the "show interface status" command at the router prompt to view your added VLANs with assigned ports. (See Figure17 below)

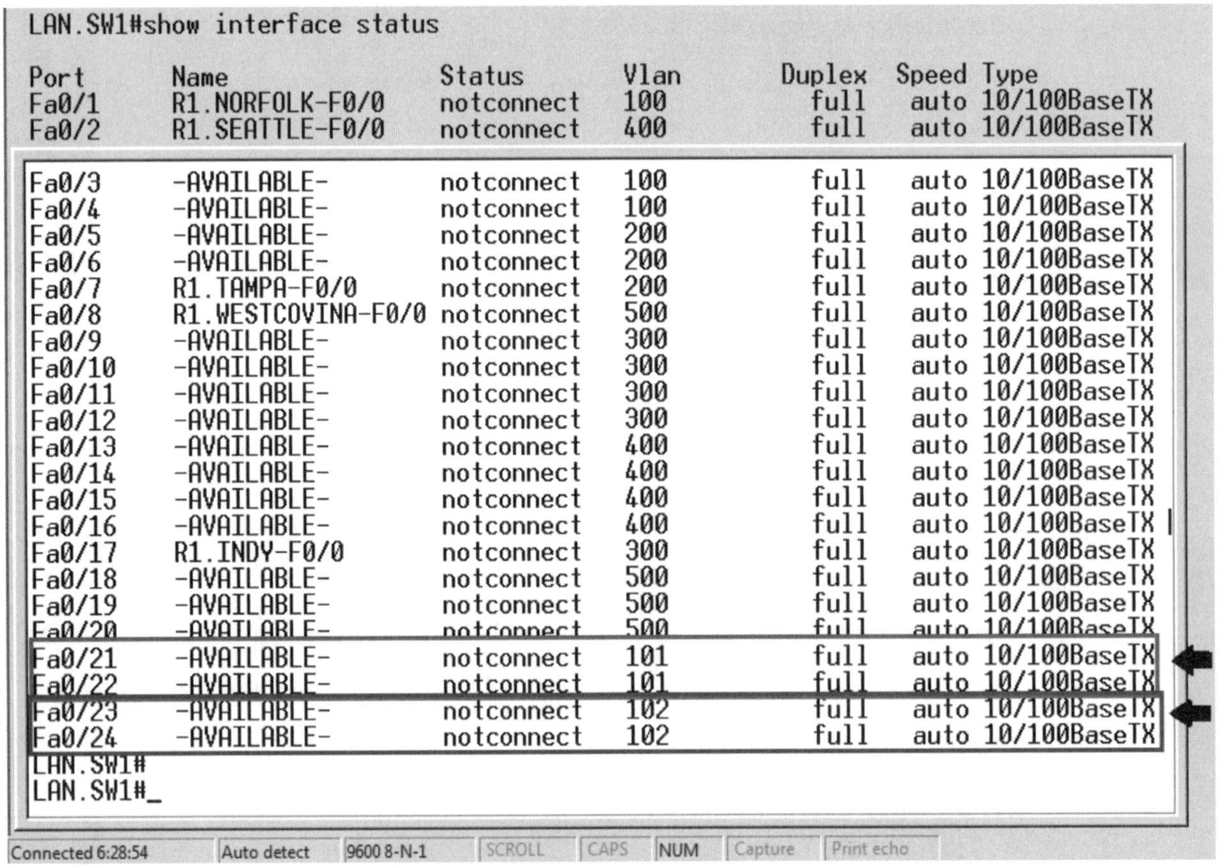

```
LAN.SW1#show interface status

Port    Name                Status      Vlan   Duplex  Speed Type
Fa0/1   R1.NORFOLK-F0/0     notconnect  100    full    auto 10/100BaseTX
Fa0/2   R1.SEATTLE-F0/0     notconnect  400    full    auto 10/100BaseTX

Fa0/3   -AVAILABLE-         notconnect  100    full    auto 10/100BaseTX
Fa0/4   -AVAILABLE-         notconnect  100    full    auto 10/100BaseTX
Fa0/5   -AVAILABLE-         notconnect  200    full    auto 10/100BaseTX
Fa0/6   -AVAILABLE-         notconnect  200    full    auto 10/100BaseTX
Fa0/7   R1.TAMPA-F0/0       notconnect  200    full    auto 10/100BaseTX
Fa0/8   R1.WESTCOVINA-F0/0  notconnect  500    full    auto 10/100BaseTX
Fa0/9   -AVAILABLE-         notconnect  300    full    auto 10/100BaseTX
Fa0/10  -AVAILABLE-         notconnect  300    full    auto 10/100BaseTX
Fa0/11  -AVAILABLE-         notconnect  300    full    auto 10/100BaseTX
Fa0/12  -AVAILABLE-         notconnect  300    full    auto 10/100BaseTX
Fa0/13  -AVAILABLE-         notconnect  400    full    auto 10/100BaseTX
Fa0/14  -AVAILABLE-         notconnect  400    full    auto 10/100BaseTX
Fa0/15  -AVAILABLE-         notconnect  400    full    auto 10/100BaseTX
Fa0/16  -AVAILABLE-         notconnect  400    full    auto 10/100BaseTX
Fa0/17  R1.INDY-F0/0        notconnect  300    full    auto 10/100BaseTX
Fa0/18  -AVAILABLE-         notconnect  500    full    auto 10/100BaseTX
Fa0/19  -AVAILABLE-         notconnect  500    full    auto 10/100BaseTX
Fa0/20  -AVAILABLE-         notconnect  500    full    auto 10/100BaseTX
Fa0/21  -AVAILABLE-         notconnect  101    full    auto 10/100BaseTX
Fa0/22  -AVAILABLE-         notconnect  101    full    auto 10/100BaseTX
Fa0/23  -AVAILABLE-         notconnect  102    full    auto 10/100BaseTX
Fa0/24  -AVAILABLE-         notconnect  102    full    auto 10/100BaseTX
LAN.SW1#
LAN.SW1#_
```

Connected 6:28:54   Auto detect   9600 8-N-1   SCROLL CAPS NUM Capture Print echo

Figure 17 - Example of the Show Interface Status Command

Current Version Date: 10/10/2011

9. Make VLAN 0101 into an extended VLAN. At the prompt enter the following:

    LAN.SW1#configure terminal

    Enter configuration commands, one per line. End with CNTL/Z.

    LAN.SW1(config)#vtp mode transparent

    Setting device to VTP TRANSPARENT mode.

    LAN.SW1(config)#vlan 0101

    LAN.SW1(config-vlan)#end

    *Mar 1 00:38:12.606: %SYS-5-CONFIG_I: Configured from console by console

    LAN.SW1#copy running-config startup-config

    Destination filename [startup-config]?

    Building configuration...

    [OK]

10. Using the PuTTY application Telnet into LAN.SW2. Login and enter the "show vlan" command.
    VLAN 0101 is present on LAN.SW2's vlan's table.

11. Telnet back into LAN.SW1. We will now configure Trunking for VLAN 0101 fast ethernet port
    fa0/21. At the prompt enter the following:

    LAN.SW1#configure terminal

    Enter configuration commands, one per line. End with CNTL/Z.

    LAN.SW1(config)#interface fa0/21

    LAN.SW1(config-if)#switchport mode dynamic auto

    LAN.SW1(config-if)#end

    LAN.SW1#

    *Mar 1 01:00:02.353: %SYS-5-CONFIG_I: Configured from console by console

    LAN.SW1#write memory

    Building configuration...

    [OK]

12. Fast ethernet port Fa0/21 on LAN.SW1is now configured for Trunking, to complete the process
    the same must be done for fast ethernet port fa0/21 on LAN.SW2. Telnet into LAN.SW2 and
    enter the following at the prompt:-

    LAN.SW2#enable

    LAN.SW2#configure terminal

    Enter configuration commands, one per line. End with CNTL/Z.

LAN.SW2(config)#interface fa0/21

LAN.SW2(config-if)#switchport mode trunk

LAN.SW2(config-if)#end

*Mar 1 00:58:02.144: %SYS-5-CONFIG_I: Configured from console by console

LAN.SW2# write memory

Note: Ethernet trunk interfaces support different trunking modes. You can set an interface as trunking or nontrunking or to negotiate trunking with the neighboring interface. To auto-negotiate trunking, the interfaces must be in the same VTP domain.

Mode	Function
switchport mode access	Puts the interface (access port) into permanent nontrunking mode and negotiates to convert the link into a nontrunk link. The interface becomes a nontrunk interface regardless of whether or not the neighboring interface is a trunk interface.
switchport mode dynamic auto	Makes the interface able to convert the link to a trunk link. The interface becomes a trunk interface if the neighboring interface is set to *trunk* or *desirable* mode. The default switchport mode for all Ethernet interfaces is **dynamic auto**.
switchport mode dynamic desirable	Makes the interface actively attempt to convert the link to a trunk link. The interface becomes a trunk interface if the neighboring interface is set to *trunk*, *desirable*, or *auto* mode.
switchport mode trunk	Puts the interface into permanent trunking mode and negotiates to convert the neighboring link into a trunk link. The interface becomes a trunk interface even if the neighboring interface is not a trunk interface.
switchport nonegotiate	Prevents the interface from generating DTP frames. You can use this command only when the interface switchport mode is **access** or **trunk**. You must manually configure the neighboring interface as a trunk interface to establish a trunk link.

13. Configure Spanning Tree Protocol (STP) and Rapid Spanning Tree Protocol(RSTP) on the Mock IT Infrastructure for each VLAN(0100, 0200, 0300, 0400 and 0500).

14. To configure STP, telnet into LAN.SW1, login and at the command prompt enter the following :

Current Version Date: 10/10/2011

LAN.SW1>enable

LAN.SW1#configure terminal

Enter configuration commands, one per line. End with CNTL/Z.

LAN.SW1(config)#spanning-tree mode pvst

LAN.SW1(config)#interface vlan0100

LAN.SW1(config-if)#spanning-tree link-type point-to-point

LAN.SW1(config-if)#end

LAN.SW1#

*Mar 1 00:35:53.632: %SYS-5-CONFIG_I: Configured from console by console

LAN.SW1#clear spanning-tree detected-protocols

LAN.SW1#show spanning-tree summary

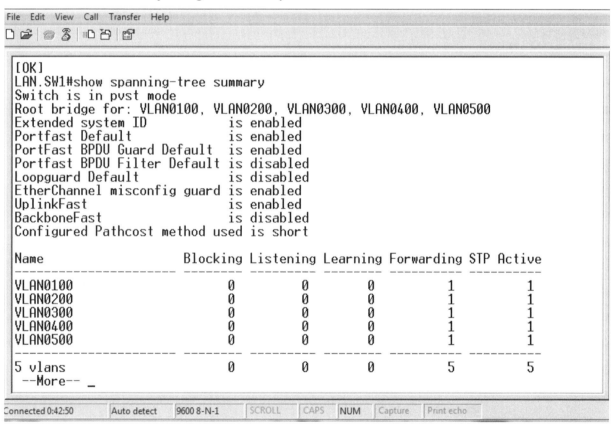

Figure 18 - Example of the Show Spanning-Tree Summary Command

15. To save changes to LAN.SW1 configuration enter the command:

LAN.SW1#copy running-config startup-config

Destination filename [startup-config]?   (just hit "ENTER" here to confirm)

Current Version Date: 10/10/2011

Building configuration...

[OK]

16. Repeat Steps 15 -16 changing the "interface " line to each corresponding VLAN e.g -

    "LAN.SW1(config)#interface vlan0100"(change value to vlan0200, then vlan0300 etc)

17. To enable Rapid Spanning Tree Protocol RSTP) enter the following commands at the prompt:

    LAN.SW1>enable

    LAN.SW1#configure terminal

    Enter configuration commands, one per line. End with CNTL/Z.

    LAN.SW1(config)#spanning-tree mode rapid-pvst

    LAN.SW1(config)#interface vlan0100

    LAN.SW1(config-if)#spanning-tree link-type point-to-point

    LAN.SW1(config-if)#end

    LAN.SW1#

    *Mar 1 00:35:53.632: %SYS-5-CONFIG_I: Configured from console by console

    LAN.SW1#clear spanning-tree detected-protocols

    LAN.SW1#show spanning-tree summary

    LAN.SW1#copy running-config startup-config

    Destination filename [startup-config]?   (just hit "ENTER" here to confirm)

    Building configuration...

    [OK]

18. Repeat Step 18 for each VLAN to enable RSTP on all VLANs.

19. Use the "show spanning-tree" command to view Spanning Tree configuration information for all

    VLANs.

Current Version Date: 10/10/2011

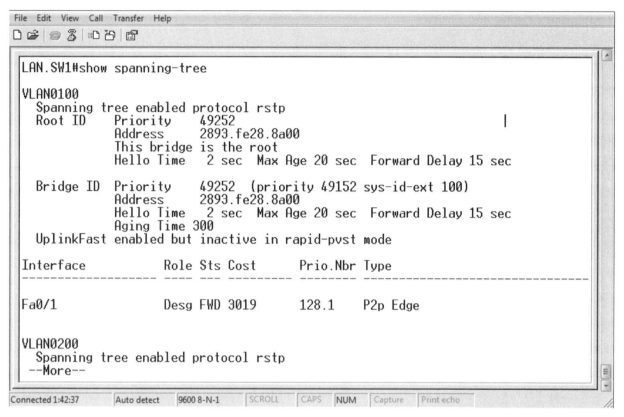

Figure 19 - Example of the Show Spanning-Tree Command

20. To test STP and RSTP students can issue a continuous ping to various Router interfaces using the "ping {ip address} -t" command. Once the ping command is executed, physically disconnect the interface connection cable to observe STP and RSTP in action.

21. Complete the Lab #6 Scenario Designing a Network Solution for a Collapsed Building Backbone, located at the end of this lab.

Deliverables

Upon completion of Lab #6: IEEE Layer 2 Networking, Virtual LANs and Resiliency, students are required to provide the following deliverables:

1. A detailed Microsoft Visio diagram of the proposed Layer 2 Networking solution for Lab #6 Scenario, Designing a Layer 2 Network Solution for a Collapsed Building Backbone

2. A Microsoft Word document explaining the proposed Layer 2 Networking solution Visio diagram for Lab #6 Scenario, Designing a Layer 2 Network Solution for a Collapsed Building Backbone

3. Lab #6 - Assessment Worksheet with answers to the assessment questions.

Evaluation Criteria and Rubrics

The following are the evaluation criteria and rubrics for Lab #6 that the students must perform:

1. Was the student able to successfully configure multiple Layer 2 Virtual LANs in a single Switch? - **[20%]**

2. Was the student able to successfully extend a Virtual LAN definition between two Switches? - **[20%]**

3. Was the student able to configure Trunk links for the extended Virtual LAN? - **[20%]**

4. Was the student able to successfully configure STP/RSTP for Layer 2 resiliency within the Mock IT infrastructure? - **[20%]**

5. Was the student able to design a Layer 2 network solution for a collapsed building backbone? - **[20%]**

Current Version Date: 10/10/2011

Lab #6 Scenario

Designing a Layer 2 Network Solution for a "Collapsed Building Backbone"

The Marketing Company Inc. management has relocated one of their remote offices to a new building in town. Their original office location had a network design tailored for a flat, level one office building, with departments strategically located in the forefront of the office building and main servers securely located in the rear. The building structure of their new office location is a three (3) story office building with a basement. The basement is only accessible by a diverted hallway door and an entrance door to the basement itself. Both doors have keypad security mechanisms.

The management of The Marketing Company Inc. has decided to have the following departmental layout with the corresponding building floors:

- **3rd Floor - Management & Accounting Departments**
- **2nd Floor - Marketing Department**
- **1st Floor - Sales/Customer Service Department**

As a Networking Specialist, The Marketing Company Inc. has contracted your skills to design a network solution which satisfies the needs and requests of management and constructing a **Layer 2 Network** design that is suitable to the physical structure of the building, whilst ensuring the efficiency and security for networking devices.

Network solution design requirements:

- Construct a detailed Visio diagram of proposed solution containing the physical layout of department workstations, cabling, routers, switches and servers.
- Microsoft Word document describing the physical layout, departmental communication and network traffic flow.

**Points to remember:

1. Departmental traffic should be segmented
2. Include and incorporate a method for network resiliency
3. Servers and networking equipment must be inaccessible to regular unauthorized personnel.
4. Solution must facilitate Layer 2 Networking.

   Hint - Research the term "collapsed backbone network**"

Lab #6 - Assessment Worksheet

IEEE Layer 2 Networking, Virtual LANs, and Resiliency

Course Name & Number: _____

Student Name: _____

Instructor Name: _____

Lab Due Date: _____

Overview

In this lab, students will learn the hands-on process of configuring multiple Layer 2 Virtual LANs on a single Switch and how to extend a Virtual LAN definition between two switches and configure Trunking. In addition, students will be introduced to Spanning Tree Protocol (STP) and Rapid Spanning Tree Protocol (RSTP) and implement it into the Mock IT infrastructure for network resiliency. Finally, students will a Design a Layer 2 network solution for a collapsed building backbone.

Lab Assessment Questions & Answers

1. What are three (3) benefits of implementing VLANs within a network?

2. What are some drawbacks of implementing VLANs within a network?

Current Version Date: 10/10/2011

3. What mode must VTP be set to on a Switch in order to extend a VLAN definition?

4. Define the term "Trunking"

5. For what purpose is Trunking used within a network?

6. What does the term STP stand for and for what purpose is it used?

7. What is the Cisco IOS command to set Spanning Tree mode to Rapid Spanning Tree Protocol?

8. Once the configuring of RSTP on Mock Infrastructure was complete and ping test was performed how much time did RSTP take to determine and implement a new path to the target destination.

9. Define the term "collapsed backbone network"

Current Version Date: 10/10/2011

Laboratory #7

Lab 7: Layer 3 Networking, Backbones, WANs & Resiliency

Learning Objectives and Outcomes

Upon completing this lab, students will be able to:

- Define functional and technical requirements for a layer 3 network.

- Design an IPv4 class-less inter-domain IP addressing and routing schema.

- Configure a IPv4 CIDR IP addressing schema for a layer 3 network.

- Design a Layer 3 network resiliency solution.

- Configure RIP on 5 remote location routers.

Required Setup and Tools

This course requires the use of the Onsite "Mock" IT Infrastructure and virtualized server farm. This is shown below:

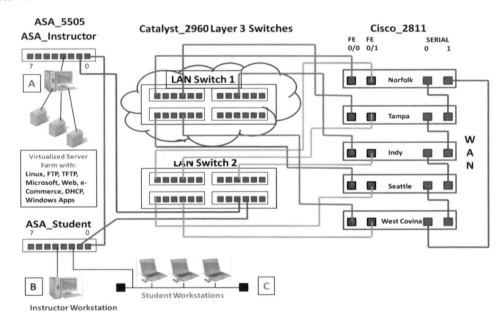

Figure 1 – Standard Onsite "Mock" IT Infrastructure & Virtualized Server Farm

The "Mock" IT Infrastructure is a preconfigured, IP network infrastructure complete with a classroom virtualized server farm. All IP addressing schema, VLAN configurations, and layer 3 switching is

Current Version Date: 10/10/2011

preconfigured. The IP networking infrastructure remains static and includes the following removable parts as indicated in Figure 1 above:

A) **NEEDED** – A classroom workstation (with at least 4 Gig RAM) capable of supporting an insert-able hard drive or USB hard drive with a preconfigured, virtualized server farm. This classroom workstation will support the virtualized VM server farm connected to the ASA_Instructor VLAN.

B) **NEEDED** – An instructor VM workstation (with at least 2 Gig RAM) that shall act as the demonstration traffic generator for the protocol capture of equipment-based labs. The Instructor will engage ARP, DHCP, ICMP, TCP 3-way handshake, FTP, HTTP, TELNET, and SSH to demonstrate protocol interaction from a preconfigured Instructor Virtual Machine (VM). The Instructor workstation/server connects to the "ASA_Student" on any of the available ports to mimic the Student's configuration. These available ports are configured to be on the same logical VLAN; hence, any port can be used. The student lab workstations connect to the same "ASA_Student" on any of the available ports.

C) **NEEDED** – Student VM workstations (with at least 2 Gig RAM) use a preconfigured Student VM to act as an Attacker VM as well as a traffic monitoring and protocol capture device. Since all the ports on the "ASA_Student" are on the same VLAN, student workstations must connect to any of the ports on the ASA5505. Students must capture the protocol interaction by generating their own unique attack traffic to their target VM in order to answer Lab #7 - Assessment Worksheet questions.

The following summarizes the setup, configuration, and equipment needed to perform Lab #7:

- Standard onsite "Mock" IT Infrastructure configuration and setup
  - Cisco 28xx routers, 29xx catalyst LAN switches, and ASA 5505 firewalls
  - TELNET accessible Cisco routers, SSH accessible Cisco routers, ICMP enabled on Cisco routers
- A virtualized server farm with:
  - A Microsoft Server VM for DHCP and other required network services
  - A "Student VM" and/or "Instructor VM" to use as the "Attacker VM" and traffic monitor
  - A "Target VM" Microsoft and/or Linux Server with the following:
    - Sample Website supporting HTTP and/or HTTPS
  - FTP and TFTP services enabled

Current Version Date: 10/10/2011

- TCP/IP protocol primer cheat sheet with well-known port numbers (Included at the end of the lab manual.)

- Standard onsite "Instructor VM" and "Student VM" must have the following software applications loaded to perform this lab:

  - VMware Player

- Standard Instructor and Student VM will be preconfigured with the following software:

  - Microsoft Word for construction and completion of Lab Scenarios.

  - Microsoft Visio for construction and completion of Lab Scenario Diagrams.

Equipment-Based Lab #7 – Student Steps:

Students should perform the following steps:

1. Insert your Student removable hard drive or USB hard drive to a classroom workstation

2. Start the VMware Player application on the classroom workstation

3. Boot up and log into your Student VM.

4. Complete Lab #7 Scenario I, Defining The Functional & Technical Requirements For A Layer 3 Network.

5. Once Lab #7 Scenario I is completed students are required to move on to the Lab #7 Scenario II, refer to Lab #7 Scenario II, Design an IPv4 Class-less Inter Domain IP Addressing & Routing Schema, located at the end of this lab.

6. Once Lab #7 Scenario II is completed move on to Lab #7 Scenario III, refer to Lab #7 Scenario III, Design a Layer 3 Network Resiliency Solution, located at the end of this lab. (Submission instructions are provided at the end of Scenario III.)

7. To learn how to enable and configure RIP on the Mock IT Infrastructure for the five (5) remote locations. Use the Cisco Core Backbone Network IP Addressing Chart, insert the IP addresses of each interface for the corresponding router after the network command for the following procedure.

8. Using PuTTy, telnet into one of the five (5) remote location Cisco 28xx routers and enter the following commands at the router prompt:- **(Note - the router R1.NORFOLK along with the corresponding IP address for each interface is being used in this example)**

   R1.NORFOLK#configure terminal

   Enter configuration commands, one per line. End with CNTL/Z.

   R1.NORFOLK(config)#router rip

Current Version Date: 10/10/2011

R1.NORFOLK(config-router)#network 172.20.0.2

R1.NORFOLK(config-router)#network 172.16.0.1

R1.NORFOLK(config-router)#network 172.16.8.1

R1.NORFOLK(config-router)#network 172.16.20.1

R1.NORFOLK(config-router)#network 172.16.1.1

R1.NORFOLK(config-router)#auto-summary

R1.NORFOLK(config-router)#end

R1.NORFOLK#write memory

*Sep 15 22:46:42.843 UTC: %SYS-5-CONFIG_I: Configured from console by cisco on console

Building configuration...

[OK]

9. To verify that the RIP protocol is configured within the Mock IT Infrastructure enter the "show ip protocols" command at the router prompt. See "Figure 1" below.

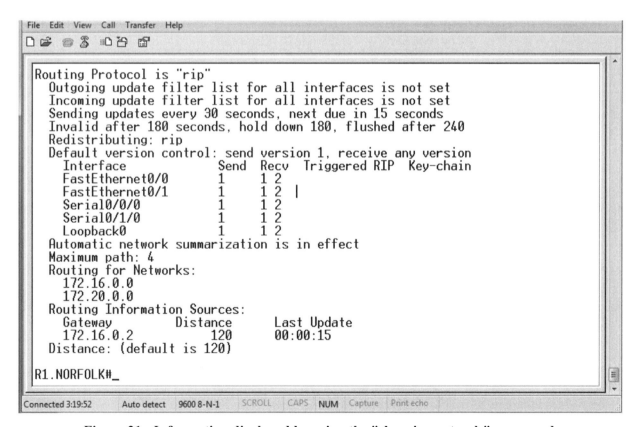

Figure 21 - Information displayed by using the "show ip protocols" command

Current Version Date: 10/10/2011

10. Telnet into each router and repeat the procedure in Step 8 to configure RIP on all location routers using the corresponding interface IP addresses found in the Cisco Core Backbone Network IP Addressing Chart.

11. Make and submit a screenshot of the "show ip protocols" command for each router labeled "*YourName* Lab#7(router name)_RIP" to the instructor.

Deliverables

Upon completion of Lab #7 Layer 3 Networking, Backbones, WANs & Resiliency, students are required to provide the following deliverables:

1. A Microsoft Visio Diagram containing the Layer 3 Solution in conjunction with a Microsoft Word document with the explanation of the Layer 3 Solution for Lab #7 Scenario I.

2. A completed IPv4 CIDR Network Table for Lab #7 Scenario II.

3. A Microsoft Visio Diagram in conjunction with a Microsoft Word document containing the Layer 3 Resiliency solution for Lab #7 Scenario III.

Evaluation Criteria and Rubrics

The following are the evaluation criteria and rubrics for Lab #7 that the students must perform:

1. Was the student able to successfully define functional and technical requirements for a layer 3 network?- **[20%]**

2. Was the student able to successfully design an IPv4 class-less inter-domain IP addressing and routing schema? - **[20%]**

3. Was the student able to successfully configure an IPv4 CIDR IP addressing schema for a layer 3 network? - **[20%]**

4. Was the student able to successfully design a layer 3 network resiliency solution? - **[20%]**

5. Was the student able to successfully configure RIP on 5 remote location routers? - **[20%]**

Current Version Date: 10/10/2011

Lab #7 Scenario I

Defining the Functional & Technical Requirements For A Layer 3 Network

The Marketing Company Inc. management has decided to implement Layer 3 Networking into the current Layer 2 network infrastructure. The management of The Marketing Company Inc. has employed the services of Network Evolutions for embark on this transitional phase. As the lead Networking Specialist and consultant you must review the current configuration (See the Network Diagram Below) and construct a report containing an analysis of the technical requirements for Layer 3 transition.

The Marketing Company Inc.'s current network infrastructure contains the following:

1. **4 Layer 2 Switches**
2. **A Network Router**
3. **A Server Farm**
4. **4 Departmental Groups of Workstations**

Rebuild the network diagram consisting of the Layer 3 implementation plan. The Layer 3 solution must:

1. **Be cost effective for the organization.**
2. **Be able to optimize network traffic whilst keeping it segmented.**
3. **Reduce the amount of network devices.**
4. **Contain a network resiliency solution**

Reconstruct the current networking infrastructure plan implementing your Layer 3 solution on a Microsoft Visio Diagram. This must be compiled with the Layer 3 Solution Report which explains the implementation and resiliency features of the proposed plan, written using Microsoft Word, Font - Times New Roman 12 pt, double spaced to submit to the instructor.

Note: Refer to the points of analysis highlighted in blue on the current network configuration to devise and construct to Layer 3 solution.

Current Version Date: 10/10/2011

-85-

Lab #7 Scenario I Diagram

The Management Company Inc. Layer 2 Networking Infrastructure

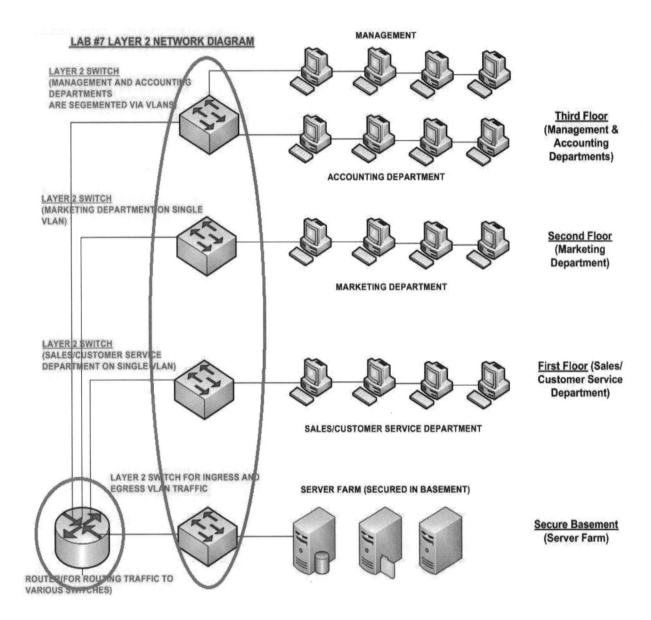

Current Version Date: 10/10/2011

Lab #7 Scenario II

Design an IPv4 Class-less Inter Domain IP Addressing & Routing Schema

The management of The Marketing Company Inc. has decided to assign their internal network to a IPv4 Class-less Inter Domain IP Addressing & Routing Schema for the network which is comprised of four departmental workgroups these are:

1. **Management Department**
2. **Marketing Department**
3. **Accounting Department**
4. **Sales & Customer Service Department**

According to the requests of The Management Company Inc. you are required to do the following:

1. **Using the IP address 172.30.0.0 and Subnet Mask of 255.255.255.0 to build your IPv4 CIDR schema. List the network address in Slash Notation.**
2. **Divide the network in four (4) subnets to facilitate 60 hosts' addresses and determine the Subnet Mask of each subnet.**
3. **List the range of each subnet (IP address of the first host and last host) and the Broadcast Address.**
4. **Determine and list the CIDR IP route number from the aggregation of the four subnets**

Refer to the online Netmatics IP Subnet & Supernetting calculator link to build the schema and using the information gathered to complete the table below:

Current Version Date: 10/10/2011

Lab #7 Scenario II Table

IPv4 CIDR Network Table

NETWORK INFORMATION						
Network Address Number of Host Addresses First Host Last Host Broadcast Address Wildcard Mask						
NETWORK SUMMARY						
Network Address & Slash Notation						
SUBNET	ADDRESS	NET MASK	HOSTS PER SUBNET	FIRST HOST	LAST HOST	BROADCAST
Subnet 1 Subnet 2 Subnet 3 Subnet 4						
CIDR ROUTE SUMMARY						

NOTE: Refer to the Netmatics IP Subnet & Supernetting Calculator link - http://www.netmatics.net/IPv4Calcs/IPv4Calcs.aspx and Tutorial on how to use the calculator - http://www.netmatics.net/IPv4Calcs/IPv4Calcs.aspx. Use the "Calculator" tab to determine the Network Information, use the "Subnetting" tab to determine information for the Network Summary section and use the "SuperNetting" calculator tab to determine the CIDR Route Summary IP address.

Current Version Date: 10/10/2011

Lab #7 Scenario III
Design a Layer 3 Network Resiliency Solution

In this scenario you will design a Layer 3 Resiliency Solution to the network infrastructure diagram below. The diagram shows a Hierarchical Layered Network Infrastructure and the communication of network devices the following layers:

- **Backbone Layer**
- **Core Layer**
- **Distribution Layer**
- **Access Layer**

Create a Layer 3 Resilience Solution for the Hierarchical Layered Network Infrastructure to provide resilience and explain how your solution will mitigate and remediate the following faults within the network configuration:

- The **VRRP Master** is down and ceases to provide network availability.

- One or more of the primary links from Layer 3 Router/Switch I **(Core Layer)** to the LAN 1, 2 or 3 Switches **(Distribution Layer)** fails.

- Links from the Layer 3 Router/Switch II **(Core Layer)** to the LAN 1,2 or 3 Switches **(Distribution Layer)** is conflicting with the primary links from Layer 3 Router/Switch I **(Core Layer)** to the LAN 1, 2 or 3 Switches **(Distribution Layer)** thus causing **topology loops** within the network. By

Current Version Date: 10/10/2011

Lab #7 Scenario III Diagram

Hierarchical Layered Network Diagram

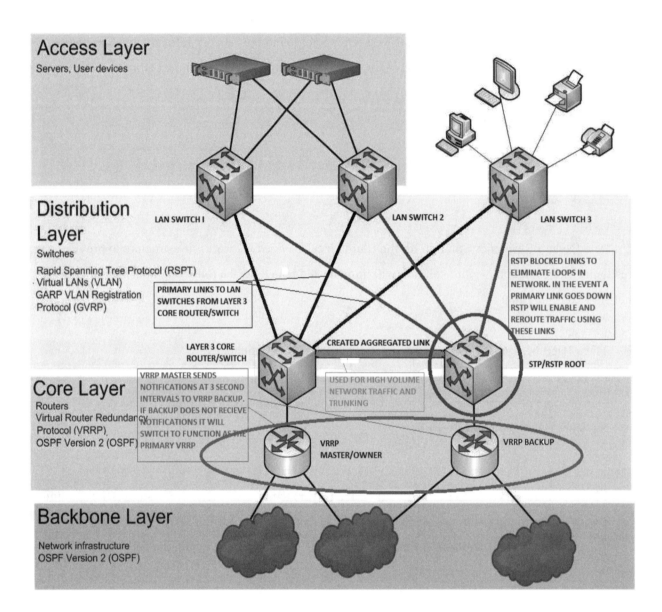

Access Layer
Servers, User devices

Distribution Layer
Switches

Rapid Spanning Tree Protocol (RSPT)
· Virtual LANs (VLAN)
GARP VLAN Registration
Protocol (GVRP)

LAN SWITCH I   LAN SWITCH 2   LAN SWITCH 3

RSTP BLOCKED LINKS TO ELIMINATE LOOPS IN NETWORK. IN THE EVENT A PRIMARY LINK GOES DOWN RSTP WILL ENABLE AND REROUTE TRAFFIC USING THESE LINKS

PRIMARY LINKS TO LAN SWITCHES FROM LAYER 3 CORE ROUTER/SWITCH

LAYER 3 CORE ROUTER/SWITCH

CREATED AGGREGATED LINK

STP/RSTP ROOT

Core Layer
Routers
Virtual Router Redundancy
Protocol (VRRP),
OSPF Version 2 (OSPF)

VRRP MASTER SENDS NOTIFICATIONS AT 3 SECOND INTERVALS TO VRRP BACKUP. IF BACKUP DOES NOT RECIEVE NOTIFICATIONS IT WILL SWITCH TO FUNCTION AS THE PRIMARY VRRP

USED FOR HIGH VOLUME NETWORK TRAFFIC AND TRUNKING

VRRP MASTER/OWNER   VRRP BACKUP

Backbone Layer
Network infrastructure
OSPF Version 2 (OSPF)

Deliverables:

A. Submit your Layer 3 Resiliency Solution on a Microsoft Visio Diagram. Replicate the given topology layout of the Hierarchical Layered Network Infrastructure and insert, proposed solutions and labels within the diagram.

B. Provide an Microsoft Word document containing the explanation of your Layer 3 Resiliency solution to address each of the three (3) faults within the network infrastructure stated above.

Current Version Date: 10/10/2011

Note - Refer to the Lab #7 Supplement Sheet, Recommended Resilient Campus Network Design: Best Practice Document, as a reference document and guide to assist in the construction of their Layer 3 Resiliency Solution.

Current Version Date: 10/10/2011

Lab #7 Supplement Sheet
IP Subnet Masks & Slash Notation

IP-Subnet-Mask numbers

IP mask numbers are used to divide internet addresses into blocks called subnets. The mask number represents the number of 1s in the binary of the address that is 'masked" against the address so that it ignores the last bits which are for the group of IP addresses in the masked address.

The first address of a subnet block (all 0s) is called the network address or network ID. The last address (all 1s) is the broadcast address of the network. Typically the network address +1 or the broadcast address -1 is the gateway to the internet. The 'slash' notation (i.e. /24) is known as CIDR format, while the more conventional 255.255.255.0 notation is considered a subnet mask.

Net bits	Subnet mask	total-addresses
/20	255.255.240.0	4096
/21	255.255.248.0	2048
/22	255.255.252.0	1024
/23	255.255.254.0	512
/24	255.255.255.0	256
/25	255.255.255.128	128
/26	255.255.255.192	64
/27	255.255.255.224	32
/28	255.255.255.240	16
/29	255.255.255.248	8
/30	255.255.255.252	4

Current Version Date: 10/10/2011

Lab #7 - Worksheet

Mock IT Infrastructure IP Addressing Schema

Mock IT Infrastructure IP Address Chart					
Router Name	**Serial 0/0**	**Serial 0/1**	**Fastethernet 0/0**	**Fastethernet 0/1**	**Loopback 0**
R1.WEST COVINA	172.19.0.2 /30	172.20.0.1 /30	172.20.8.1 /24	172.20.20.1 /24	172.20.1.1 /32
Description	R1.SEATTLE-S 0/1	R1.NORFOLK-S 0/1	DMZ-LAN-SW1-FE0/16	TRUST-LAN-SW2-FE0/16	
Router Name	**Serial 0/0**	**Serial 0/1**	**Fastethernet 0/0**	**Fastethernet 0/1**	**Loopback 0**
R1.SEATTLE	172.18.0.2 /30	172.19.0.1 /30	172.19.8.1 /24	172.19.20.1 /24	172.19.1.1 /32
Description	R1.INDY-S 0/1	R1.WESTCOVINA-S 0/0	DMZ-LAN-SW1-F0/2-V400	TRUST-LAN-SW2-F0/2-V401	
Router Name	**Serial 0/0**	**Serial 0/1**	**Fastethernet 0/0**	**Fastethernet 0/1**	**Loopback 0**
R1.INDY	172.17.0.2 /30	172.18.0.1 /30	172.18.8.1 /24	172.18.20.1 /24	172.18.1.1 /32
Description	R1.TAMPA-S 0/1	R1.SEATTLE-S 0/0	DMZ-LAN-SW1-F0/17-V300	TRUST-LAN-SW2-F0/17-V301	
Router Name	**Serial 0/0**	**Serial 0/1**	**Fastethernet 0/0**	**Fastethernet 0/1**	**Loopback 0**
R1.TAMPA	172.16.0.2 /30	172.17.0.1 /30	172.17.8.1 /24	172.17.20.1 /24	172.17.1.1 /32
Description	R1.NORFOLK-S 0/1	R1.INDY-S 0/0	DMZ-LAN-SW1-F0/7-V200	TRUST-LAN-SW2-F0/7-V201	
Router Name	**Serial 0/0**	**Serial 0/1**	**Fastethernet 0/0**	**Fastethernet 0/1**	**Loopback 0**
R1.NORFOLK	172.20.0.2 /30	172.16.0.1 /30	172.16.8.1 /24	172.16.20.1 /24	172.16.1.1 /32
Description	R1.WEST COVINA-S 0/1	R1.TAMPA-S 0/0	DMZ-LAN-SW1-FE0/1	TRUST-LAN-SW2-FE0/1	
Switch Name	**Vlan 100**	**Fastethernet 0/1**	**Fastethernet 0/2**	**Fastethernet 0/7**	**Fastethernet 0/8**
LAN.SW1	172.16.8.5 /24				
Description		R1.NORFOLK-F 0/0	R1.SEATTLE-F 0/0	R1.TAMPA-F0/0	R1.WEST COVINA-F0/0
Switch Name	**Vlan 101**	**Fastethernet 0/1**	**Fastethernet 0/2**	**Fastethernet 0/7**	**Fastethernet 0/8**
LAN.SW2	172.16.20.5 /24				
Description		R1.NORFOLK-F 0/1	R1.SEATTLE-F 0/1	R1.TAMPA-F0/1	R1.WEST COVINA-F0/1
ASA Name	**Vlan2 "Inside"**	**Vlan501 "Outside"**	**Vlan600 "DMZ"**		
ASA-Student	172.31.0.1 /24 (IP Default GW)	172.20.20.10 /24	172.29.0.2 /24		
Description	Can only ping this from vlan2.	Can ping this from outside.	Cannot ping this from outside.		
ASA Name	**Vlan2 "Inside"**	**Vlan501 "Outside"**	**Vlan600 "DMZ"**		
ASA-Instructor	172.30.0.1 /24 (IP Default GW)	172.20.20.11 /24	172.29.0.1 /24		
Description	Can ony ping this from vlan2.	Can ping this from outside.	Cannot ping this from outside.		

Current Version Date: 10/10/2011

Lab #7 - Assessment Worksheet
Layer 3 Networking, Backbones, WANs & Resiliency

Course Name & Number: _____

Student Name: _____

Instructor Name: _____

Lab Due Date: _____

Overview

In this lab, students will learn complete various scenarios for defining functional and technical requirements for a layer 3 network using models current of real world implementations and solutions. Students will design an IPv4 class-less inter-domain IP addressing and routing schema and configure it for Layer 3 networking using online resources and tools such as calculators for IP addressing, Subnetting and Supernetting. In addition to being introduced to various Layer 3 protocols (RIP) and methods and implementing them for Layer 3 Resiliency planning and remote WAN solution building.

Lab Assessment Questions & Answers

1. Define the term "Subnetting"?

2. Define the term "Supernetting"?

Current Version Date: 10/10/2011

3. Define the term Network Resiliency?

4. How does the Virtual Router Redundancy Protocol (VRRP) utilized to ensure network redundancy?

5. Name three (3) dynamic routing protocols that can be used to distribute routing information?

6. What is meant by the term Class-less Inter Domain Routing (CIDR)?

7. What protocol/s can be used to eliminate loops in network topology?

8. What is the function of GARP VLAN Registration Protocol (GVRP)?

Current Version Date: 10/10/2011

9. What is the function of the Link Aggregation Control Protocol (LACP)?

10. What does RIP stand for and what is its function?

11. What is the command used to configure RIP on the Cisco 28xx routers and what mode must be enabled to execute the command?

Current Version Date: 10/10/2011

Laboratory #8

Lab 8: Distance Vector IP Routing, Building & Campus Backbones, WANs & Classful IP Routing

Learning Objectives and Outcomes

Upon completing this lab, students will be able to:

- Distinguish Classful VS. Classless inter-domain IP Routing

- Align routing metrics to different distance Vector routing protocols.

- Configure a Layer 3 resiliency for a Layer 3 network to solve availability challenges.

- Configure RIPv2 IP routing protocol for a Layer 3 network to solve alternate path availability.

- Configure EIGRP IP routing protocol for a Layer 3 network to solve alternate path availability for LAN & WAN.

Required Setup and Tools

This course requires the use of the Onsite "Mock" IT Infrastructure and virtualized server farm. This is shown below:

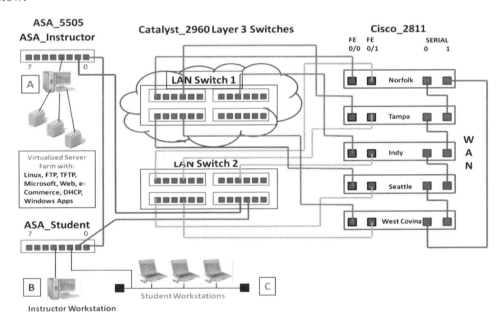

Figure 1 – Standard Onsite "Mock" IT Infrastructure & Virtualized Server Farm

The "Mock" IT Infrastructure is a preconfigured, IP network infrastructure complete with a classroom virtualized server farm. All IP addressing schema, VLAN configurations, and layer 3 switching is

preconfigured. The IP networking infrastructure remains static and includes the following removable parts as indicated in Figure 1 above:

A) **NEEDED** – A classroom workstation (with at least 4 Gig RAM) capable of supporting an insert-able hard drive or USB hard drive with a preconfigured, virtualized server farm. This classroom workstation will support the virtualized VM server farm connected to the ASA_Instructor VLAN.

B) **NEEDED** – An instructor VM workstation (with at least 2 Gig RAM) that shall act as the demonstration traffic generator for the protocol capture of equipment-based labs. The Instructor will engage ARP, DHCP, ICMP, TCP 3-way handshake, FTP, HTTP, TELNET, and SSH to demonstrate protocol interaction from a preconfigured Instructor Virtual Machine (VM). The Instructor workstation/server connects to the "ASA_Student" on any of the available ports to mimic the Student's configuration. These available ports are configured to be on the same logical VLAN; hence, any port can be used. The student lab workstations connect to the same "ASA_Student" on any of the available ports.

C) **NEEDED** – Student VM workstations (with at least 2 Gig RAM) use a preconfigured Student VM to act as an Attacker VM as well as a traffic monitoring and protocol capture device. Since all the ports on the "ASA_Student" are on the same VLAN, student workstations must connect to any of the ports on the ASA5505. Students must capture the protocol interaction by generating their own unique attack traffic to their target VM in order to answer Lab #8 - Assessment Worksheet questions.

The following summarizes the setup, configuration, and equipment needed to perform Lab #8:

- Standard Onsite "Mock" IT Infrastructure configuration and setup
  - Cisco 28xx routers, 29xx catalyst LAN switches, and ASA 5505 firewalls
  - TELNET accessible Cisco routers, SSH accessible Cisco routers, ICMP enabled on Cisco routers
- A virtualized server farm with:
  - A Microsoft Server VM for DHCP and other required network services
  - A "Student VM" and/or "Instructor VM" to use as the "Attacker VM" and traffic monitor
  - A "Target VM" Microsoft and/or Linux Server with the following:
    - Sample Website supporting HTTP and/or HTTPS

Current Version Date: 10/10/2011

- FTP and TFTP services enabled
- TCP/IP protocol primer cheat sheet with well-known port numbers (Included at the end of the lab manual.)
- Standard onsite Instructor VM and Student VM must have the following software applications loaded to perform this lab:
  - VMware Player
- Standard Instructor and Student VM will be preconfigured with the following software:
- Microsoft Word for construction and completion of Lab Scenarios.

Equipment-Based Lab #8 – Student Steps:

Students should perform the following steps:

1. Insert your Student removable hard drive or USB hard drive to a classroom workstation
2. Start the VMware Player application on the classroom workstation
3. Boot up and log into your Student VM.
4. Using the information from Lab #8 Exercise I, Classful vs Classless Inter-Domain IP Routing, complete the Classful VS Classless Inter-Domain Routing Comparison Table by identifying the differences in Classful vs Classless inter-domain IP Routing characteristics. Lab #8 Exercise I and the Comparison Table can be found at the end of this lab.
5. Move on to the next lab objective - Aligning routing metrics to various Distance Vector routing protocols
6. Open an Internet Explorer or Mozilla Firefox browsing window and research the following Distance Vector Protocols:
   - **Static Routing**
   - **Routing Information Protocol (RIP)**
   - **Routing Information Protocol Version II (RIPV2)**
   - **Interior Gateway Routing Protocol (IGRP)**
   - **Enhanced Interior Gateway Routing Protocol (EIGRP)**
7. Using the information gathered from the research complete Lab #8 Exercise II by inserting arrows from first column (Protocol Name) to the correct corresponding description in second column (Features & Metrics). Lab #8 Exercise II can be found at the end of this lab.
8. Move on to the next lab objective - Designing a Layer 3 Resiliency for a Layer 3 Network to solve availability challenges

Current Version Date: 10/10/2011

9. You will now learn how to enable and configure RIPV2 on the Mock IT Infrastructure for the five (5) remote locations. Using the Cisco Core Backbone Network IP Addressing Chart, insert the IP addresses of each interface for the corresponding router after the "**network**" command for the following procedure.

10. Using PuTTy, telnet into one of the five (5) remote location Cisco 28xx routers and enter the following commands at the router prompt: **(Note - the router R1.NORFOLK along with the corresponding network IP address for each interface is being used in this example)**

    R1.NORFOLK#

    R1.NORFOLK#enable

    R1.NORFOLK#configure terminal

    Enter configuration commands, one per line. End with CNTL/Z.

    R1.NORFOLK(config)#router rip

    R1.NORFOLK(config-router)#version 2

    R1.NORFOLK(config-router)#network 172.20.0.0

    R1.NORFOLK(config-router)#network 172.16.0.0

    R1.NORFOLK(config-router)#network 172.16.8.0

    R1.NORFOLK(config-router)#network 172.16.20.0

    R1.NORFOLK(config-router)#network 172.16.1.0

    R1.NORFOLK(config-router)#no auto-summary

    R1.NORFOLK(config-router)#end

    R1.NORFOLK#

    *Sep 19 03:38:23.203 UTC: %SYS-5-CONFIG_I: Configured from console by cisco on console

    R1.NORFOLK#write memory

    Building configuration...

    [OK]

11. To verify that the RIPV2 protocol is configured within the Mock IT Infrastructure enter the "**show ip protocols**" command at the router prompt. See following "Figure 21".

Current Version Date: 10/10/2011

-100-

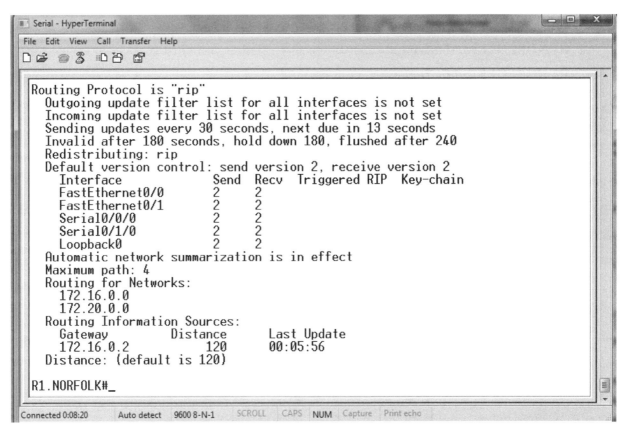

Figure 22 - Information Displayed by Using the "show ip protocols" Command

12. Telnet into each router and repeat the procedure in Step 10 to configure RIPV2 on all location routers using the corresponding interface network IP addresses found in the Cisco Core Backbone Network IP Addressing Chart

13. Submit a screenshot of the "show ip protocols" command for each router labeled "*YourName* Lab#8(router name)_RIPV2" to the instructor.

14. You will now learn how to enable and configure EIGRP on the Mock IT Infrastructure for the five (5) remote locations. Using the Cisco Core Backbone Network IP Addressing Chart, insert the IP addresses of each interface for the corresponding router after the "network" command for the following procedure.

15. Using PuTTy, telnet into one of the five (5) remote location Cisco 28xx routers and enter the following commands at the router prompt:- **(Note - the router R1.NORFOLK along with the corresponding IP address for each interface is being used in this example)**

    R1.NORFOLK#enable

    R1.NORFOLK#configure terminal

Current Version Date: 10/10/2011

Enter configuration commands, one per line. End with CNTL/Z.

R1.NORFOLK(config)#router eigrp 100

R1.NORFOLK(config-router)#no auto-summary

R1.NORFOLK(config-router)#network 172.20.0.0

R1.NORFOLK(config-router)#network 172.16.0.0

R1.NORFOLK(config-router)#network 172.16.8.0

R1.NORFOLK(config-router)#network 172.16.20.0

R1.NORFOLK(config-router)#network 172.16.1.0

R1.NORFOLK(config-router)#end

R1.NORFOLK#

*Sep 19 05:20:45.943 UTC: %SYS-5-CONFIG_I: Configured from console by cisco on console

R1.NORFOLK#write memory

Building configuration...

[OK]

16. To verify that the EIGRP is configured within the Mock IT Infrastructure enter the "show ip protocols" command at the router prompt. See following "Figure 23".

Current Version Date: 10/10/2011

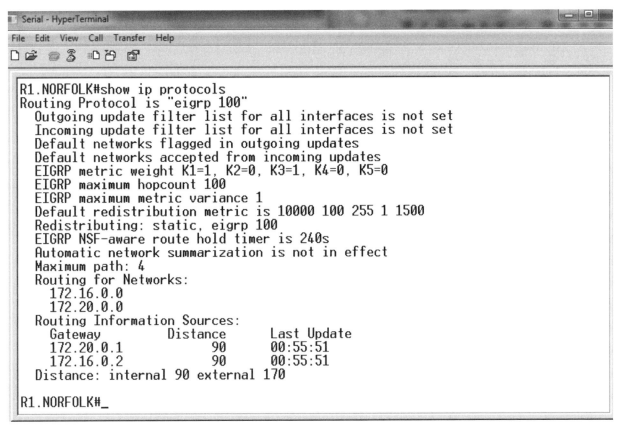

Figure 23 - EIGRP Configuration Displayed by Using the "show ip protocols" Command

17. Telnet into each router and repeat the procedure in Step 15 to configure EIGRP on all location routers using the corresponding interface network IP addresses found in the Cisco Core Backbone Network IP Addressing Chart

18. Submit a screenshot of the "show ip protocols" command for each router labeled "*YourName* Lab#8(router name)_EIGRP" to the instructor.

Deliverables

Upon completion of Distance Vector IP Routing, Building & Campus Backbones, WANs & Classful IP Routing, students are required to provide the following deliverables as part of this lab:

1. The completed Lab #8 Exercise I, Classful vs Classless Inter-Domain Routing Comparison table for "*YourName* Lab #8 Exercise I"

2. The completed Lab #8 Exercise II, Aligning Distance Vector Routing Protocols table for "*YourName* Lab #8 Exercise II"

3. A Microsoft Word document containing the Layer 3 Resiliency solution report for the Mock IT Infrastructure for "*YourName* Lab #8 Scenario I"

4. Labeled screen capture files displaying the "show ip protocols" command for RIPV2 router configuration.

5. Labeled screen capture files displaying the "show ip protocols" command for EIGRP router configuration.

Evaluation Criteria and Rubrics

The following are the evaluation criteria and rubrics for Lab #8 that the students must perform:

1. Was the student able to successfully distinguish Classful vs Classless inter-domain IP Routing? - **[20%]**

2. Was the student able to successfully align routing metrics to different distance Vector routing protocols? - **[20%]**

3. Was the student able to successfully design layer 3 resiliency for a layer 3 network to solve availability challenges? - **[20%]**

4. Was the student able to successfully configure RIPv2 IP routing protocol for a layer 3 network to solve alternate path availability? - **[20%]**

5. Was the student able to successfully configure EIGRP IP routing protocol for a layer 3 network to solve alternate path availability for LAN & WAN? - **[20%]**

Current Version Date: 10/10/2011

Lab #8 Exercise I

Classful vs Classless Inter-Domain IP Routing

In this exercise students will learn to distinguish between Classful and Classless Inter-Domain IP routing. The tables below (Table 1.1 & Table 1.2) contains the network information for:

- A network using a Class C IP addressing scheme **192.168.0.1** Netmask -**255.255.255.0**

- A network using a Class B IP addressing scheme **172.16.0.1** Netmask - **255.255.0.0**

NETWORK INFORMATION	NETWORK VALUES
Class C Address	192.168.0.1
Netmask	255.255.255.0
Network Address	192.168.0.0
Total Number of Host Addresses	254
First Host Address	192.168.0.1
Last Host Address	192.168.0.254
Broadcast Address	192.168.0.255
Wildcard Mask	0.0.0.255

Table 1.1 - Displaying Class C network information

NETWORK INFORMATION	NETWORK VALUES					
Class B Address	172.16.0.1					
Netmask	255.255.0.0					
Network Address	172.16.0.0					
Total Number of Host Addresses	65536					
Allocated Subnets	4					
SUBNET INFORMATION						
Subnet	Address	Mask	Hosts	First Host	Last Host	Broadcast
Subnet1	172.16.0.0	255.255.192.0	16382	172.16.0.1	172.16.63.254	172.16.63.255
Subnet2	172.16.64.0	255.255.192.0	16382	172.16.64.1	172.16.127.254	172.16.127.255
Subnet3	172.16.128.0	255.255.192.0	16382	172.16.128.1	172.16.191.254	172.16.191.255
Subnet4	172.16.192.0	255.255.192.0	16382	172.16.192.1	172.16.255.254	172.16.255.255

Table 1.2 - Displaying Class B network information

Compare the network characteristics of the two tables and determine the network using Classful Routing from the network using Classless Inter-Domain Routing. Identify and list three (3) differences of Classful and Classless Inter-Domain Routing characteristics you identified from the network information displayed in the tables above and complete the table below:

Current Version Date: 10/10/2011

Lab #8 Exercise I

Classful VS Classless Inter-Domain Routing Comparison Table

	Classful Inter-Domain Routing	Class-less Inter-Domain Routing
1		
2		
3		

Current Version Date: 10/10/2011

Lab #8 Exercise II
Distance Vector Protocol Table

PROTOCOL		FEATURES & METRICS
1	Static Routing	Due to the deficiencies of the original specification, this protocol was developed with the ability to carry subnet information supporting Classless Inter-Domain Routing (CIDR). To maintain backward compatibility, the hop count limit of 15 remained.
2	Routing Information Protocol (RIP)	is a data communication concept describing one way of configuring path selection achieved by manually adding routes to the routing table. This type of configuration is not fault tolerant. When there is a change in the network or a failure occurs traffic will not be rerouted.
3	Routing Information Protocol Version II (RIPV2)	is an advanced distance-vector routing protocol, with optimizations to minimize both the routing instability incurred after topology changes, as well as the use of bandwidth and processing power in the router. There are five (5) K values used in the Composite metric calculation - K1 through K5. The K values only act as multipliers or modifiers in the composite metric calculation.
4	IGRP	is the original specification of the protocol which uses classful single routing metric and a maximum hop count limit of 15. Routing updates do not carry subnet information, lacking support for variable length subnet masks (VLSM). This limitation makes it impossible to have different sized subnets inside of the same network class.
5	Enhanced Interior Gateway Routing Protocol (EIGRP)	is a proprietary protocol created to overcome the limitations of RIP. It supports multiple metrics for each route, including bandwidth, delay, load, MTU, and reliability. The maximum hop count of routed packets is 255 (default 100), and routing updates are broadcast every 90 seconds (by default).

Current Version Date: 10/10/2011

Lab #8 Scenario I

Mock IT Infrastructure Resiliency Methods

In this scenario you will identify and explain methods in which the Mock IT Infrastructure can be configured for network resilience to solve availability challenges. Refer to the diagram below of the network infrastructure and identify resiliency methods which can be implemented to counteract the following:

- **Ethernet link physical damage or loss in connectivity between the various Cisco 28xx location routers. (NORKFOLK, TAMPA, SEATTLE, INDY & WEST COVINA)**

- **WAN serial connection failures or loss in connectivity between the various Cisco 28xx location routers. (NORKFOLK, TAMPA, SEATTLE, INDY & WEST COVINA)**

- **Network loops due to poorly configured network topology arrangement.**

- **Failure of one or more of the Cisco 28xx routers(NORKFOLK, TAMPA, SEATTLE, INDY & WEST COVINA)**

- **Degradation of network performance due to non-segmented network traffic between devices.**

For each of the preceding instances identify resilience methods with can be implemented within the Mock IT Infrastructure to remediate and solve network availability challenges. Explain how each of the selected methods can work within the infrastructure to provide network resiliency.

Deliverables

Submit a report on the various resiliency methods which can be implemented to solve availability challenges for the Mock IT Infrastructure on a Microsoft Word document, Font 12 pt Times New Roman, Double-spaced to the instructor.

Current Version Date: 10/10/2011

Lab #8 Scenario I Diagram

Diagram of the Mock IT Infrastructure

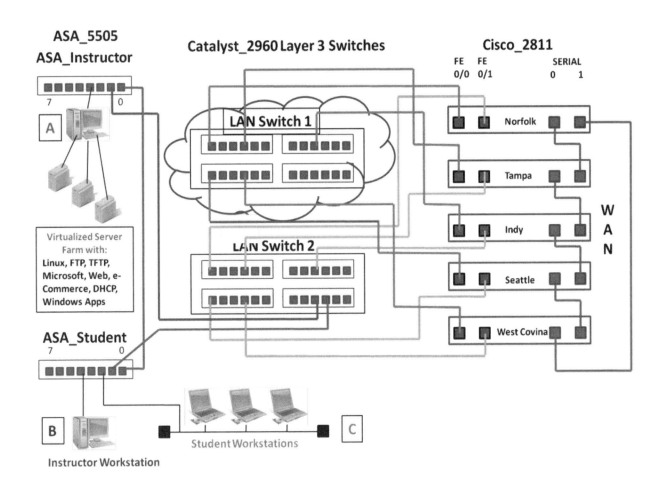

Note: Research STP/RSTP, VRRP, RIP/RIPV2 and EIRGP protocols and how they work within the network infrastructure to assist them in building their solution for the Mock IT Infrastructure.

Current Version Date: 10/10/2011

Lab #8 - Assessment Worksheet

Distance Vector IP Routing, Building & Campus Backbones, WANs
& Classful IP Routing

Course Name & Number: _____

Student Name: _____

Instructor Name: _____

Lab Due Date: _____

Overview

In this lab students, through research, will learn to distinguish Classful vs Classless Inter-Domain IP Routing and align routing metrics to different distance Vector routing protocols. Configure layer 3 resiliency for a layer 3 network to solve availability challenges on the Mock IT Infrastructure using routing protocols such as RIP,STP, EIRGP etc. Following by the actually performing the live configuration of RIPv2 IP and EIGRP IP routing protocols for a Layer 3 network to solve alternate path availability and provide resiliency for LAN & WAN infrastructure.

Lab Assessment Questions & Answers

1. What is meant by the term Classful Routing?

2. What are three (3) characteristics of Classful IP Routing?

Current Version Date: 10/10/2011

3. What are three (3) characteristics of Classless Inter-Domain IP Routing?

4. Define the term Network Resiliency?

5. What does EIGRP stand for and what is its function?

6. What does RIP stand for and what is its function?

7. Which routing protocol uses a maximum hop count of 15 for IP routing?

Current Version Date: 10/10/2011

8. Which routing protocol uses K values in its composite metric calculations for IP routing?

9. EIGRP was created due to the drawbacks of IGRP such as routing updates are not able to carry subnet information and lack of support for variable length subnet masks(VLSM). True or False?

10. EIGRP can be used on LAN & WAN environments as a resiliency method to maintain network availability. True or False?

Current Version Date: 10/10/2011

Laboratory #9

Lab #9: OSPF - Network Design - OSPFv2 for IPv4 and OSPF v3 for IPv6

Learning Objectives and Outcomes

Upon completing this lab, students will be able to correctly:

- Design an OSPFv2 hierarchical network to support a given IPv4 network design and topology

- Select an IPv4 addressing scheme to support a given network design and topology

- Specify the OSPFv2 areas and maximum number of subnets and hosts per area

- Develop an OSPFv2 to OSPFv3 migration strategy to support expansion and growth

- Design an OSPFv3 hierarchical network to support a give IPv6 network design and topology

- Convert a given IPv4 addressing scheme to an IPv6 addressing scheme to support a given network design and topology

- Develop the appropriate Cisco OSPF router configuration commands to support a given 2-layer hierarchical network design, IP addressing, and topology scheme for both IPv4 and IPv6

Required Setup and Tools

This is a paper-based lab and does not require the use of the "Mock" IT infrastructure or virtualized server farm.

- The standard Student Microsoft Windows workstation with Microsoft Office 2007 or higher, with Microsoft Word for Lab #9 – Assessment Worksheet Questions.

Paper-Based Lab #9 – Student Steps:

The following presents the steps needed to perform Lab #9 OSPF - Network Design - OSPFv2 for IPv4 and OSPF v3 for IPv6. The management of the Complex Company Inc. has decided to redesign their internal network for their six building campus network. Contracting the services of Network Evolutions Inc., They have submitted the following requirements:

- Build an IPv4 addressing scheme for the six building campus network

- The IP addressing schema must be "Class B" (172.32.0.0)

- OSPFv2 is the routing protocol

- Assume subnet 0 is supported

- Each campus building has 32 departments with up to 136 workstations each

Current Version Date: 10/10/2011

- Each of the campus building areas must be on different subnets respectively

- IP addresses will be assigned beginning with campus building Area 101, then 102 through 106, and finally the core router interconnections,

- Core routers are all fully meshed connected

1. Determine the IP address to be used and its Class

2. Determine the IP network subnet mask required to support the Complex Company's network design

3. Determine OSPF areas required

4. Starting with OSPF Area 101:

    a. List the subnetwork numbers for this OSPF area,

    b. For the first and last subnetwork within this OSPF area, define:

        i. The IP subnetwork number,

        ii. The first host IP address,

        iii. The last host IP address, and

        iv. The IP broadcast address.

5. For OSPF Areas 102 through 105:

    a. List the subnetwork numbers assigned to each in a summary format 172.32.X.0 thru 172.32.Y.0

6. For OSPF Area 106:

    a. List the subnetwork numbers for this OSPF area,

    b. For the first and last subnetwork within this OSPF area, define:

        i. The IP subnetwork number,

        ii. The first host IP address,

        iii. The last host IP address, and

        iv. The IP broadcast address.

7. For the Core router RTR-A:

    a. Determine how many subnetworks are needed to interconnect the core routers?

    b. Determine how many hosts are required per subnetwork?

    c. Determine the subnetwork mask that should be used within the core?

    d. Determine the first subnetwork number assigned within the core?

    e. Determine the first IP address assigned to a host within this subnet?

Current Version Date: 10/10/2011

    f.   Determine the last IP address assigned to a host within this subnet?

    g.   Determine the broadcast IP address for this subnet?

    h.   Determine the last subnetwork number assigned within the core?

    i.   Determine the first IP address assigned to a host within this subnet?

    j.   Determine the last IP address assigned to a host within this subnet?

    k.   Determine the broadcast IP address for this subnet?

8. For Core router RTR-A, develop the appropriate Cisco OSPFv2 router configuration commands to support IPv4 within this network topology.

9. For Core router RTR-A, determine how one might simplify the number of network statements needed to specify the subnetwork addresses supported within Area 101 and Area 0 both for routing and advertising.

10. Determine the limitations a Class B IP address solution. (Subnetworks, hosts, network growth, etc.).

11. Develop a migration strategy for implementing to OSPFv3 IPv6 if the network where to add more campus buildings and/or departments to the network.

12. Assume the IPv6 address assigned to the Complex Company is 2002:2:0:0/64. .

13. For Core router RTR-A, develop the appropriate Cisco OSPFv3 router configuration commands to support both IPv4 and IPv6 within this network topology.

14. Be prepared to defend your decision.

15. Answer the Lab #9 – Assessment Worksheet questions.

Note: Students can refer to the Lab #9 IP Schema Network Design Diagram sheet for visual reference. You can also use the link to the online subnetting calculator to assist in building your scheme:

http://subnet-calculator.com/subnet.php?net_class=B

and the IPv4 to IPv6 Calculator

http://www.subnetonline.com/pages/subnet-calculators/ipv4-to-ipv6-converter.php

---

Deliverables

Upon completion of Lab #9: OSPF - Network Design - OSPFv2 for IPv4 and OSPF v3 for IPv6, students are required to provide the following deliverables as part of this lab:

As a Network Engineer for Network Evolutions Inc., you must configure an OSPF backbone to provide the requirements for the management of The Complex Company Inc. campus buildings and answer the following:

1. Lab #9 – Explain your migration plan for implementing OSPFv2 within the Complex Company's network.

2. Lab #9 – For the first and last campus buildings (Area 101 and 106):
   a. The first host IPv4 address, the last host IPv4 address, and the IPv4 broadcast address for the first and last subnetwork.

3. Lab #9 – For Core Router RTR-A:
   a. The first host IPv4 address, the last host IPv4 address, and the IPv4 broadcast address for the first and last subnetwork.

4. Lab #9 – For Core Router RTR-A, list the OSPFv2 IPv4 configuration commands needed for your solution.

5. Lab #9 – Explain the limitations that exist within the OSPFv2 IPv4 solution that you have created.

6. Lab #9 – Explain your migration plan for the OSPFv2 IPv4 to OSPFv3 IPv6 conversion.

7. Lab #9 – IPv4 to IPv6 conversion:
   a. The first and last subnetwork address for Area 101
   b. The first and last subnetwork address for Area 106

8. Lab #9 – For Core Router RTR-A, list the OSPFv3 IPv6 configuration commands need for your solution.

9. Lab #9 – Assessment Worksheet with answers to the assessment questions

Students are to complete the answers on a Word Document, Times New Roman font size 12, regular.

Evaluation Criteria and Rubrics

The following are the evaluation criteria and rubrics for Lab #9 OSPF - Network Design - OSPFv2 for IPv4 and OSPF v3 for IPv6 that the students must perform:

1. Was the student able to correctly articulate the processes necessary to create an IPv4 OSPFv2 network? – **[20%]**

2. Was the student able to correctly select an IPv4 addressing scheme to support the given network design and topology? – **[10%]**

3. Was the student able to correctly specify the OSPFv2 areas and maximum number of subnets and hosts per area? – **[10%]**

4. Was the student able to correctly develop an OSPFv2 to OSPFv3 migration strategy to support expansion and growth? – **[20%]**

5. Was the student able to correctly design an OSPFv3 hierarchical network to support a give IPv6 network design and topology? – **[10%]**

6. Was the student able to correctly convert a given IPv4 addressing scheme to an IPv6 addressing scheme to support a given network design and topology? – **[10%]**

7. Was the student able to correctly develop the appropriate Cisco OSPF router configuration commands to support a given 2-layer hierarchical network design, IP addressing, and topology scheme for both IPv4 and IPv6? – **[20%]**

Lab #9 – Complex Company, Inc. Network Topology

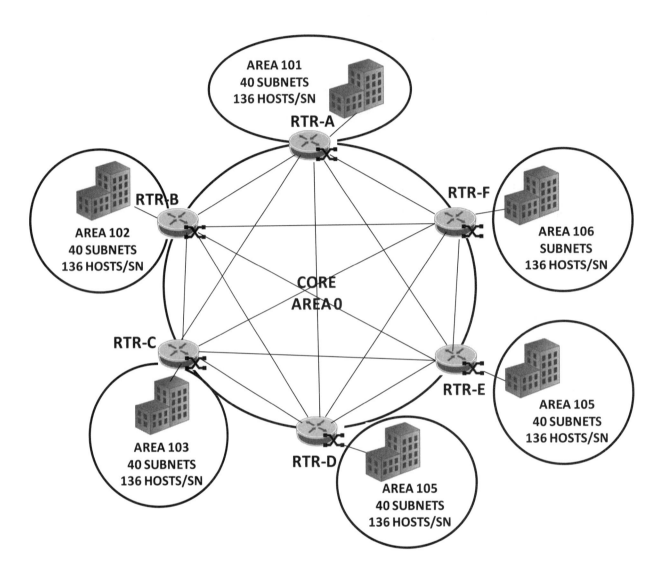

Current Version Date: 10/10/2011

Subnet and Host Bits

Mask Value	Mask Size in Bits	Maximum Hosts	Subnets / Class A	Subnets / Class B	Subnets / Class C
255.0.0.0	8	16,777,214	1	0	0
255.128.0.0	9	8,388,606	0	0	0
255.192.0.0	10	4,194,302	2	0	0
255.224.0.0	11	2,097,150	6	0	0
255.240.0.0	12	1,048,574	14	0	0
255.248.0.0	13	524,286	30	0	0
255.252.0.0	14	262,142	62	0	0
255.254.0.0	15	131,070	126	0	0
255.255.0.0	16	65,534	254	1	0
255.255.128.0	17	32,766	510	0	0
255.255.192.0	18	16,382	1,022	2	0
255.255.224.0	19	8,190	2,046	6	0
255.255.240.0	20	4,094	4,094	14	0
255.255.248.0	21	2,046	8,190	30	0
255.255.252.0	22	1,022	16,382	62	0
255.255.254.0	23	510	32,766	126	0
255.255.255.0	24	254	65,534	254	1
255.255.255.128	25	126	131,070	510	0
255.255.255.192	26	62	262,142	1,022	2
255.255.255.224	27	30	524,286	2,046	6
255.255.255.240	28	14	1,048,574	4,094	14
255.255.255.248	29	6	2,097,150	8,190	30
255.255.255.252	30	2	4,194,302	16,382	62

Current Version Date: 10/10/2011

Lab #9 - Assessment Worksheet Questions

OSPF - Network Design - OSPFv2 for IPv4 and OSPF v3 for IPv6

Course Name & Number: _____

Student Name: _____

Instructor Name: _____

Lab Due Date: _____

Explain your migration plan for implementing OSPFv2 within the Complex Company's network:

Current Version Date: 10/10/2011

For IPv4 answer the following:

1. Class B IP Address

2. Maximum amount of campus building Subnets

3. The Subnet mask for the campus building areas

4. The number of total IP addresses that each subnet can facilitate

5. The host IP address ranges within each campus building subnet

6. The Subnet ID

7. The Broadcast Address

For the first subnet within OSPF area 101:

1. What is the subnetwork number assigned?

2. What is the IP address of the first host within this subnet?

3. What is the last IP address assigned to a host within this subnet?

4. What is the broadcast IP address for this subnet?

For the last subnet within OSPF area 101:

1. What is the subnetwork number assigned?

2. What is the IP address of the first host within this subnet?

3. What is the last IP address assigned to a host within this subnet?

4. What is the broadcast IP address for this subnet?

For the first subnet within OSPF area 106:

1. What is the subnetwork number assigned?

2. What is the IP address of the first host within this subnet?

3. What is the last IP address assigned to a host within this subnet?

4. What is the broadcast IP address for this subnet?

For the last subnet within OSPF area 106:

1. What is the subnetwork number assigned?

2. What is the IP address of the first host within this subnet?

3. What is the last IP address assigned to a host within this subnet?

4. What is the broadcast IP address for this subnet?

Current Version Date: 10/10/2011

For the Core routers:

1. How many subnetworks are required to interconnect the core routers?

2. How many hosts are required per subnetwork within the core?

3. What subnetwork mask should be used within the core?

4. What is the first subnetwork number assigned within the core?

5. What is the first IP address assigned to a host within this subnet?

6. What is the last IP address assigned to a host within this subnet?

7. What is the broadcast IP address for this subnet?

8. What is the IP last subnetwork address assigned within the core?

9. What is the first IP address assigned to a host within this subnet?

10. What is the last IP address assigned to a host within this subnet?

11. What is the broadcast IP address for this subnet?

For Core Router RTR-A, list the OSPFv2 IPv4 configuration commands needed for your solution:

Current Version Date: 10/10/2011

1. Explain the command "Network 172.32.0.0 0.0.31.255 area 101"

2. Explain the command "area 101 range 172.32.0.0 255.255.224.0"

Explain the limitations that exist within the OSPFv2 IPv4 solution that you have created.

Explain your migration plan for the OSPFv2 IPv4 to OSPFv3 IPv6 conversion.

Current Version Date: 10/10/2011

In order to migrate from an IPv4 to an IPv6 based network, you must define an IPv6 addressing scheme.

The Complex Company was assigned 2002:2:0:0/64 as their IPv6 base address.

For this lab, we are only going to be concerned with IPv6 addresses for Core router RTR-A.

Develop an addressing scheme for the Core Area 0 routers and Area 101 routers. An IPv6 address has the following format:

001	Global Routing Prefix	Subnet	Interface Address

$$\longleftarrow \quad 48 \quad \longrightarrow \!\!\times\!\! \longleftarrow 16 \longrightarrow\!\!\times\!\! \longleftarrow \quad 64 \quad \longrightarrow$$

1. The advantage of IPv6 is the number of subnet bits available. How many subnets are available?

2. This equates to how many subnets?

We know that all IP addressing within an OSPF area must be contiguous, we should increase the number of subnets available within an area to handle future growth.
Arbitrarily, let's increase each area to 64 subnetworks.

3. If we begin with the Core Area 0, what would be the range for IPv6 address?

4. What would the range of IPv6 addresses in Area 101?

Current Version Date: 10/10/2011

For Core Router RTR-A, list the OSPFv3 IPv6 configuration commands needed for your solution to support a dual stack IPv4 and IPv6 OSPFv3 transition network.

Current Version Date: 10/10/2011

Laboratory #10

Lab 10: Network Management – FCAPS

Learning Objectives and Outcomes

Upon completing this lab, students will be able to:

- Design an SNMP Fault Management and alarming solution.

- Utilize Spiceworks as an Asset Management solution.

- Design an SNMP Performance Management solution for capacity planning.

- Implement Security Management and controls throughout the IP network Infrastructure.

- Craft a Change Control procedure definition.

Required Setup and Tools

This course requires the use of the Onsite "Mock" IT Infrastructure and virtualized server farm. This is shown below:

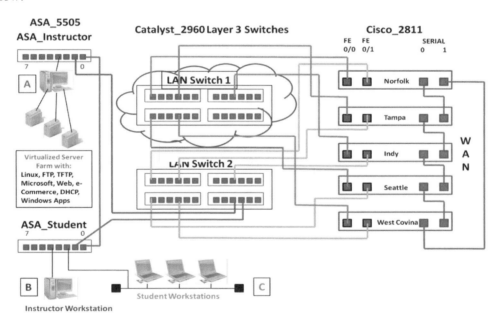

Figure 1 – Standard Onsite "Mock" IT Infrastructure & Virtualized Server Farm

The "Mock" IT Infrastructure is a preconfigured, IP network infrastructure complete with a classroom virtualized server farm. All IP addressing schema, VLAN configurations, and layer 3 switching is

Current Version Date: 10/10/2011

preconfigured. The IP networking infrastructure remains static and includes the following removable parts as indicated in Figure 1 above:

A) **NEEDED** – A classroom workstation (with at least 4 Gig RAM) capable of supporting an insert-able hard drive or USB hard drive with a preconfigured, virtualized server farm. This classroom workstation will support the virtualized VM server farm connected to the ASA_Instructor VLAN.

B) **NEEDED** – An instructor VM workstation (with at least 2 Gig RAM) that shall act as the demonstration traffic generator for the protocol capture of equipment-based labs. The Instructor will engage ARP, DHCP, ICMP, TCP 3-way handshake, FTP, HTTP, TELNET, and SSH to demonstrate protocol interaction from a preconfigured Instructor Virtual Machine (VM). The Instructor workstation/server connects to the "ASA_Student" on any of the available ports to mimic the Student's configuration. These available ports are configured to be on the same logical VLAN; hence, any port can be used. The student lab workstations connect to the same "ASA_Student" on any of the available ports.

C) **NEEDED** – Student VM workstations (with at least 2 Gig RAM) use a preconfigured Student VM to act as an Attacker VM as well as a traffic monitoring and protocol capture device. Since all the ports on the "ASA_Student" are on the same VLAN, student workstations must connect to any of the ports on the ASA5505. Students must capture the protocol interaction by generating their own unique attack traffic to their target VM in order to answer Lab #10 - Assessment Worksheet questions.

The following summarizes the setup, configuration, and equipment needed to perform Lab #10:

- Standard Onsite "Mock" IT Infrastructure configuration and setup
  - Cisco 28xx routers, 29xx catalyst LAN switches, and ASA 5505 firewalls
  - TELNET accessible Cisco routers, SSH accessible Cisco routers, ICMP enabled on Cisco routers
- A virtualized server farm with:
  - A Microsoft Server VM for DHCP and other required network services
  - A "Student VM" and/or "Instructor VM" to use as the "Attacker VM" and traffic monitor
  - A "Target VM" Microsoft and/or Linux Server with the following:
    - Sample Website supporting HTTP and/or HTTPS
  - FTP and TFTP services enabled

Current Version Date: 10/10/2011

- TCP/IP protocol primer cheat sheet with well-known port numbers (Included at the end of the lab manual.)

- Standard onsite Instructor and Student VM must have the following software applications loaded to perform this lab:

  - VMware Player

- Standard Instructor and Student VM will be preconfigured with the following software:

  - Internet Explorer or Mozilla Firefox for downloading the "Spiceworks" application.

  - Spiceworks application - used for management of SNMP, Availability & Performance reporting within the Mock IT Infrastructure.

  - TFTped application for transferring of files between network devices.

  - PuTTy application to initiate telnet sessions to various network devices.

Equipment-Based Lab #10 – Student Steps:

Students should perform the following steps:

1. Insert your Student removable hard drive or USB hard drive to a classroom workstation

2. Start the VMWare Player application on the classroom workstation

3. Boot up and log into your Student VM.

4. Open a new browser window and navigate to the Spiceworks download page - http://www.spiceworks.com/ download and install the Spiceworks application.

5. Divide into Teams as per the Instructor request.

6. Using the PuTTY application Telnet into the Mock IT Infrastructure's networking devices - 2 Cisco Catalyst 29xx Switches and the five (5) Cisco 28xx Location Routers (LAN SW1, LAN SW2, RI.NORFOLK, R1.TAMPA, RI.INDY, R1.SEATTLE & R1.WEST COVINA) and enter the following commands to enable and configure **SNMP** logging.

7. To configure SNMP logging on a Cisco 28xx Router enter the following at the command prompt:

    R1.INDY#**configure terminal**

    Enter configuration commands, one per line. End with CNTL/Z.

    R1.INDY(config)#**snmp-server community public ro**

    R1.INDY(config)#**snmp-server host 172.31.0.xx 255.255.255.0** *(in this line enter your host IP address)*

    R1.INDY(config)#**end**

Current Version Date: 10/10/2011

*Sep 21 15:42:59.659 UTC: %SYS-5-CONFIG_I: Configured from console by cisco on c

onsole

R1.INDY#**write memory**

Building configuration...

[OK]

8. To verify that SNMP logging has been enabled and active on the configured router enter the

    "**show snmp**" command. See Figure 24 below:

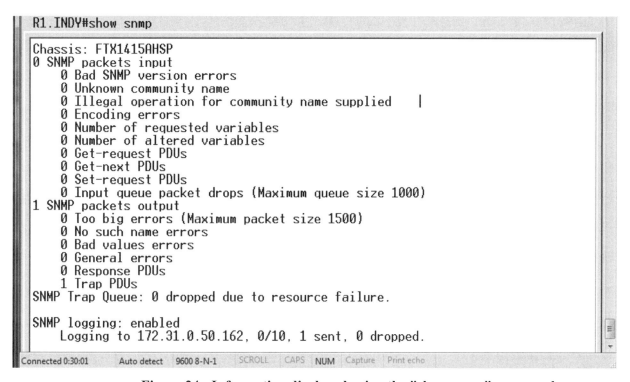

```
R1.INDY#show snmp
Chassis: FTX1415AHSP
0 SNMP packets input
    0 Bad SNMP version errors
    0 Unknown community name
    0 Illegal operation for community name supplied    |
    0 Encoding errors
    0 Number of requested variables
    0 Number of altered variables
    0 Get-request PDUs
    0 Get-next PDUs
    0 Set-request PDUs
    0 Input queue packet drops (Maximum queue size 1000)
1 SNMP packets output
    0 Too big errors (Maximum packet size 1500)
    0 No such name errors
    0 Bad values errors
    0 General errors
    0 Response PDUs
    1 Trap PDUs
SNMP Trap Queue: 0 dropped due to resource failure.

SNMP logging: enabled
    Logging to 172.31.0.50.162, 0/10, 1 sent, 0 dropped.
```

Connected 0:30:01   Auto detect   9600 8-N-1   SCROLL   CAPS **NUM** Capture   Print echo

Figure 24 - Information displayed using the "show snmp" command

9. To configure SNMP logging on Cisco 29xx Switch enter the following at the command prompt:

    LAN.SW1#**configure terminal**

    Enter configuration commands, one per line. End with CNTL/Z.

    LAN.SW1(config)#**snmp-server community public ro**

    LAN.SW1(config)#**snmp-server host 172.31.0.xx 255.255.255.0** *(in this line enter your*

    host IP address)

    LAN.SW1(config)#*snmp-server enable traps*

    LAN.SW1(config)#**end**

LAN.SW1#

*Mar 1 01:52:11.169: %SYS-5-CONFIG_I: Configured from console by console

LAN.SW1#write memory

Building configuration...

[OK]

10. To verify that SNMP logging has been enabled and active on the configured switch enter the "show snmp" command. See figure below:

```
LAN.SW1#show snmp
Chassis: FOC1411226X
0 SNMP packets input
    0 Bad SNMP version errors
    0 Unknown community name
    0 Illegal operation for community name supplied
    0 Encoding errors
    0 Number of requested variables
    0 Number of altered variables
    0 Get-request PDUs
    0 Get-next PDUs
    0 Set-request PDUs
    0 Input queue packet drops (Maximum queue size 1000)
1 SNMP packets output
    0 Too big errors (Maximum packet size 1500)
    0 No such name errors
    0 Bad values errors
    0 General errors
    0 Response PDUs
    1 Trap PDUs
SNMP global trap: enabled

SNMP logging: enabled
    Logging to 172.31.0.50.162, 1/10, 0 sent, 0 dropped.
SNMP agent enabled
LAN.SW1#_
```

11. Install the Spiceworks application on your VM and use the following steps for configuration for SNMP management :

Example of the Spiceworks application boot screen

12. Enter your *first, last, email address and password* on the Login credential screen.

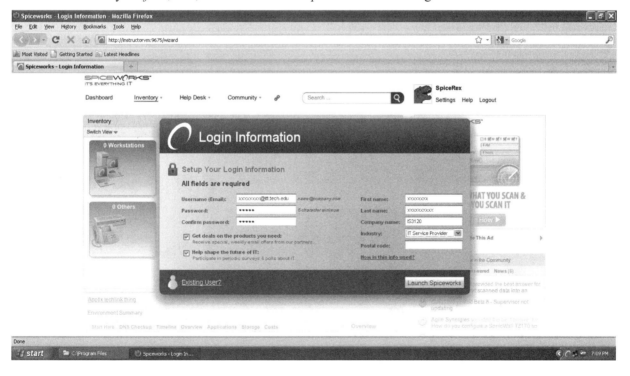

Current Version Date: 10/10/2011

13. Select "**Inventory**" on the "**Where Would You Like to Start**" screen.

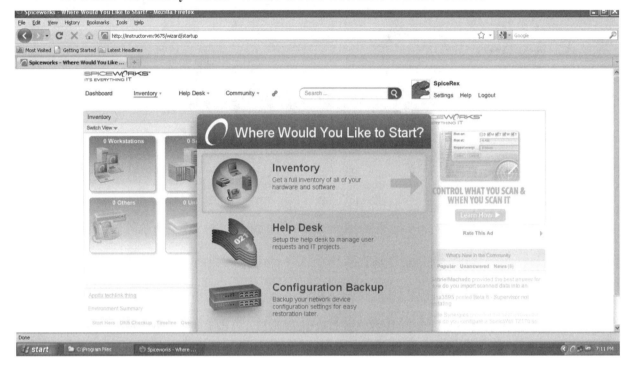

Selections present on the "Where You Would Like to Start" screen

14. Enter the network range "**172.31.0.1-254**" to scan for the entire host network.

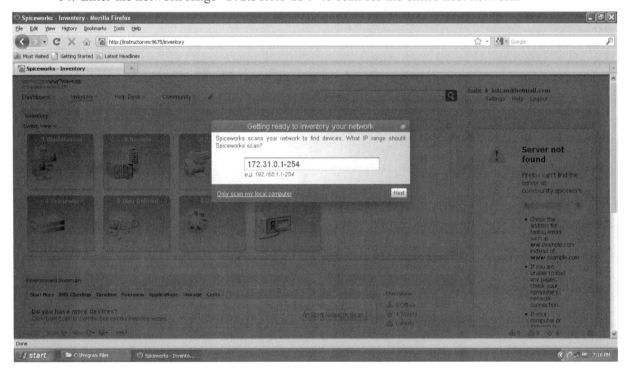

Current Version Date: 10/10/2011

15. On the "Scan Settings" screen leave settings at default and hit **"Start Scan"**.

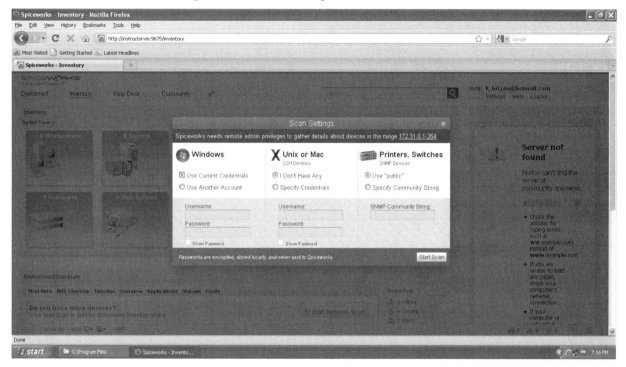

16. One the scan is completed, navigate to **"Inventory"**, and click **"Settings"**.

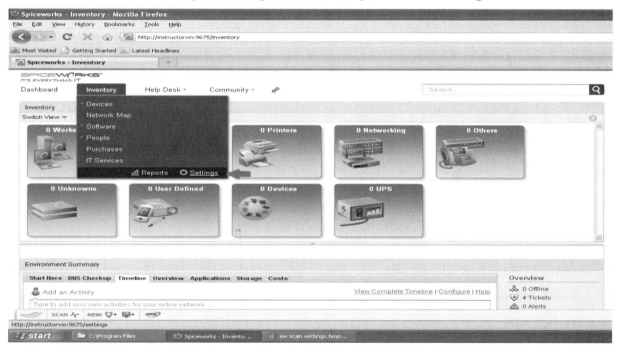

Current Version Date: 10/10/2011

17. Navigate to and click "**Network Scan**" on the "Settings" page.

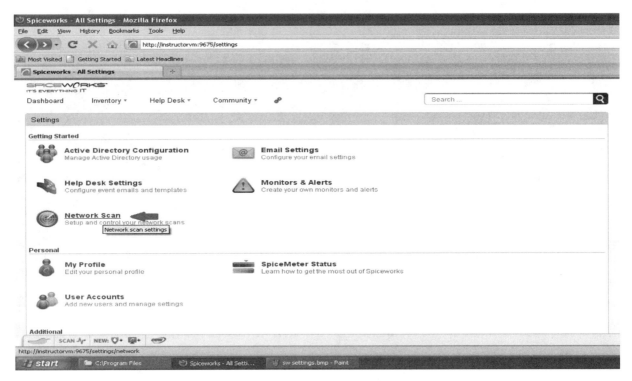

Navigating to the "Network Scan" tab under the "Settings" menu

18. At the "**Add New Scan Entry**" box using the " Mock IP Addressing Scheme" handout enter the IP address of a selected network device - 2 Cisco Catalyst 29xx Switches and the five (5) Cisco 28xx Location Routers (LAN SW1, LAN SW2, RI.NORFOLK, R1.TAMPA, RI.INDY, R1.SEATTLE & R1.WEST COVINA)

19. For the "**Windows**" and "**SSH**" account fields enter select "**NONE**" from the drop down box.

20. For the "**SNMP**" account field select "**Public**" and click save.

21. Repeat Steps 18 - 20 entering all the IP addresses for the interfaces and loopback for each network device.

Current Version Date: 10/10/2011

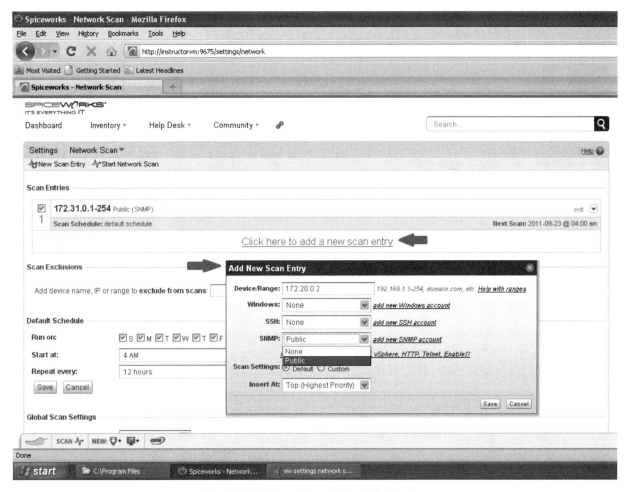

The "Add A New Scan Entry" dialog box

22. Once all IP interface addresses for all network devices are entered saved click the **"Start Network** Scan" tab.

Current Version Date: 10/10/2011

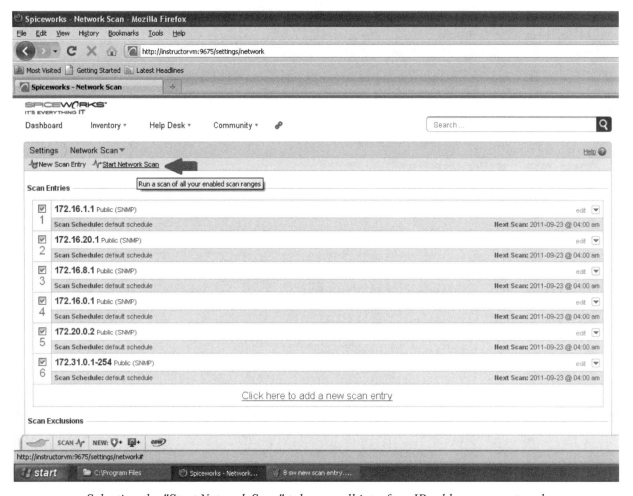

Selecting the "Start Network Scan" tab once all interface IP address are entered

23. Once the scan is completed navigate to the "**Inventory**" and select "**Network Map**" to view a diagram of the network containing all devices discovered by the Network Scan.

Current Version Date: 10/10/2011

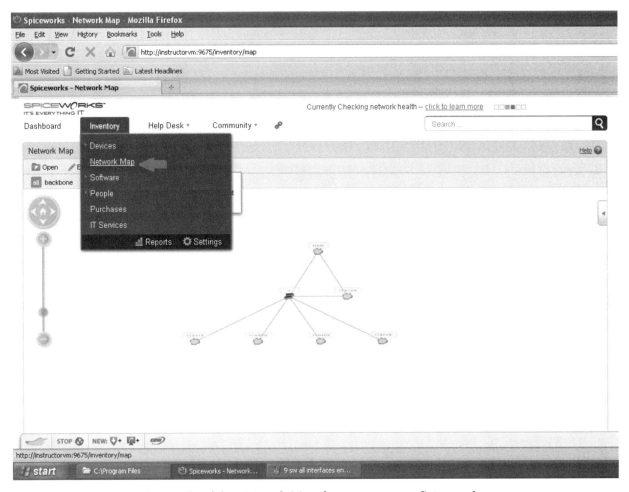

Example of the Network Map diagram in using Spiceworks

24. Return to the "**Inventory**" tab and click "**Settings**". From the "**Settings**" page select "**Monitors & Alerts**".

Current Version Date: 10/10/2011

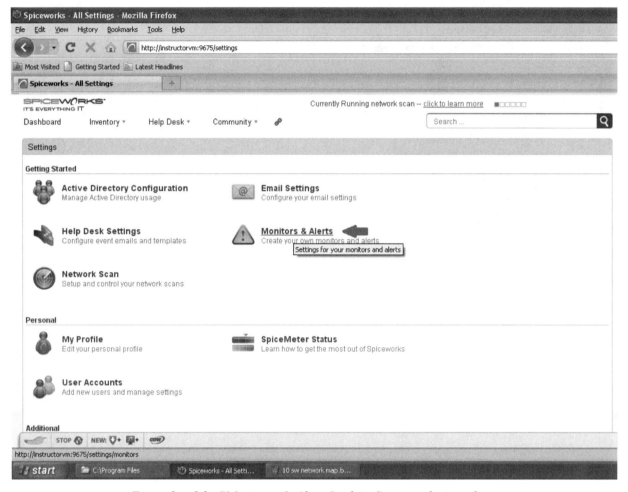

Example of the "Monitors & Alerts" tab in Spiceworks interface

25. In the "**Monitors & Alerts**" screen a list of preconfigured alerts with be enabled by default.

26. Remove the check marks in the boxes for "**Enable**" and "**Email**" for all preconfigured alerts excluding the "**Any Device - configuration changed - Networking**" alert.

Current Version Date: 10/10/2011

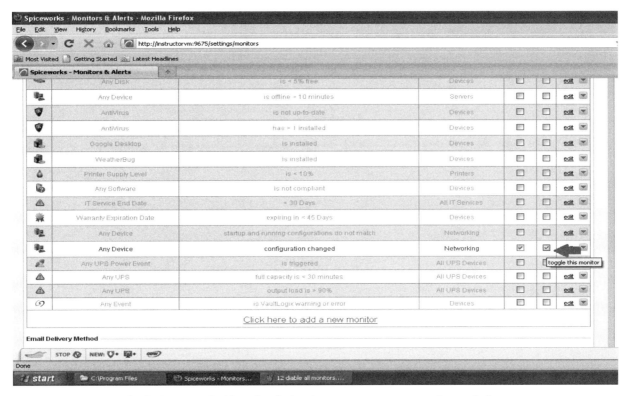

The "Monitors & Alerts" tab displaying various preconfigured alerts

27. Scroll to the bottom of the list and click on the "Click here to add a new monitor" tab.

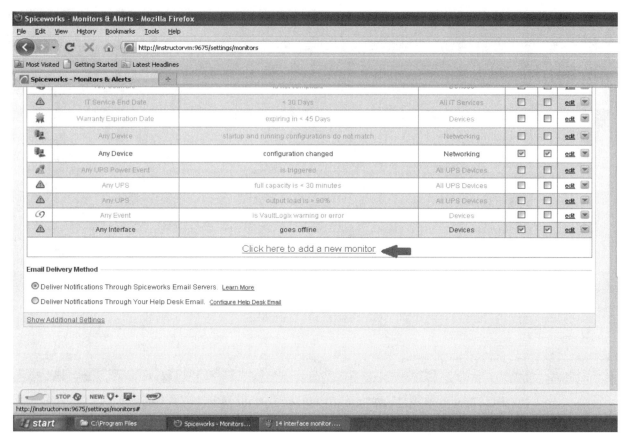

Selecting the "Click here to add a new monitor" tab

28. Under the "**Add a New Monitor**" field enter the following to configure an alert for if any interface on any network device goes offline. Select the following from the drop down box in the fields:

   TYPE: **Interface**

   NAME: *(leave blank to apply to all devices)*

   CONDITION: **goes offline**

   APPLIES TO: **Devices**

29. Ensure that the check mark boxes for "**Email**" and "**Enabled**" are checked and click "**save**".

Current Version Date: 10/10/2011

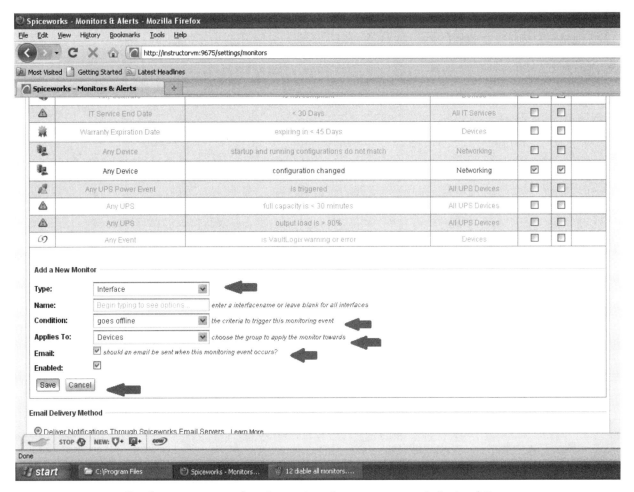

Configuring a new alert for an interface on a network device failure

30. Under the "**Add a New Monitor**" field enter the following to configure an alert for if any network device goes offline. Select the following from the drop down box in the fields:

    TYPE: **Device**

    NAME: *(leave blank to apply to all devices)*

    CONDITION: **is offline**

    APPLIES TO: **Devices**

31. Ensure that the check mark boxes for "**Email**" and "**Enabled**" are checked and click "**save**".

32. Return to the "**Inventory**" tab and click on "**Devices**".

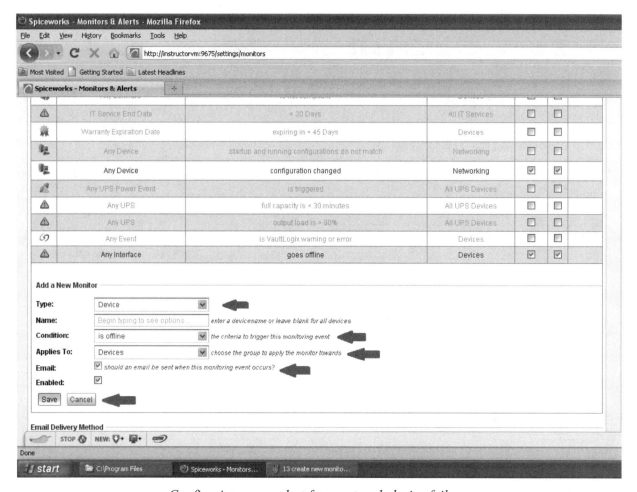

Configuring a new alert for a network device failure

33. To test the newly configured alerts, power off a network device and disconnect fastethernet and Serial links for other devices that are still powered on.

34. Within a few seconds new alert notifications will appear on the bottom right of the Spiceworks interface window.

35. Navigate to your email inbox to verify that email notifications for alerts are present.

Current Version Date: 10/10/2011

Spiceworks interface displaying offline alert notifications

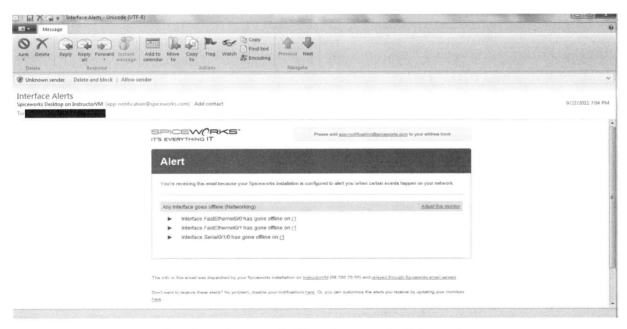

Email notification of offline alerts sent by Spiceworks

36. To generate reports for implementing Security Management and controls throughout the IP network infrastructure use the "**Reports**" tab.

37. Navigate to the "**Inventory**" tab and select "**Reports**"

Selecting the "Reports" tab under "Inventory"

38. Have students perform 5-10 minutes of following to generate network statistics:

- **Pinging to workstations and network devices**

- **TFTP files to workstations**

- **Internet Browsing sessions**

- **Disconnecting and reconnection Ethernet and serial links on various network devices**

39. Return to the "**Reports**" tab to view a list of various preconfigured reports.

40. Select a report from the list to determine the "**Average Network Bandwidth Utilization**".

41. Select **"run"** from the "**Actions**" column.

42. Once the report is generated, select the desired format to save and submit to the instructor.

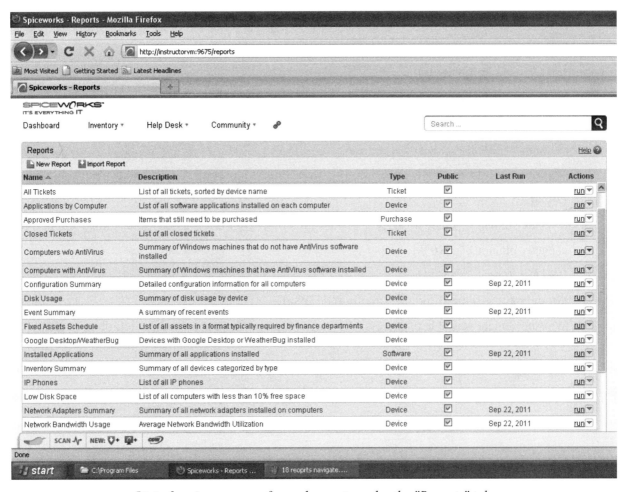

List of various pre-configured reports under the "Reports" tab

Note: You can also create customized New Reports with selected criteria using the "New Report" tab to generate network statistics for any situation.

Deliverables

Upon completion of the Network Management – FCAPS lab, students are required to provide the following deliverables:

1. A softcopy of the Average Network Bandwidth Utilization Report generated by Spiceworks.
2. A Microsoft Word document containing the completed six (6) phases of a Change Control Procedure definition.

Evaluation Criteria and Rubrics

The following are the evaluation criteria and rubrics for Lab #10 that the students must perform:

1. Was the student was able to successfully design an SNMP Fault Management and alarming solution? - **[20%]**
2. Was the student was able to successfully utilize Spiceworks as an Asset Management solution? - **[20%]**
3. Was the student was able to successfully design an SNMP Performance Management solution for capacity planning? - **[20%]**
4. Was the student was able to successfully implement Security Management and controls throughout the IP network infrastructure? - **[20%]**
5. Was the student was able to successfully craft a Change Control procedure definition? - **[20%]**

Current Version Date: 10/10/2011

Lab #10 Scenario I

Crafting a Change Control Procedure Definition

In this scenario you will learn the fundamentals of the Change Control process by building a Change Control Procedure Definition. There are six (6) stages that map out the ordered course of how a procedure should be executed. The diagram below displays the flow process of these stages:

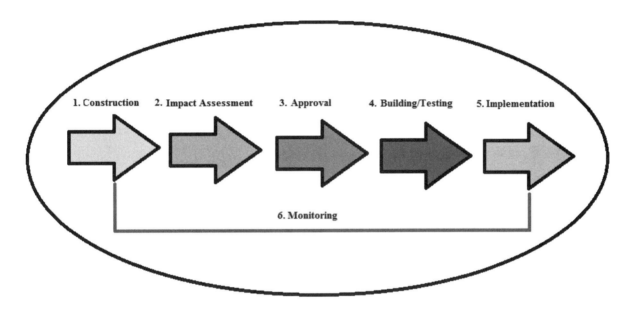

Change Control Procedure Flowchart

1. **Construction/Request -**

2. **Impact Assessment -**

3. **Approval -**

Current Version Date: 10/10/2011

4. **Building/Testing -**

5. **Implementation -**

6. **Monitoring -**

Describe how processes are performed at each of the six (6) stages. Include persons, groups, processes and decisions involved within the organization which defines how a Change Control Procedure is executed. Craft your Change Control Definition on a Microsoft Word Document, 12 pt font, double-spaced and submit to the instructor.

Note: Refer to Chapter Six (6) of the "Fundamentals of Information Systems Security" text book for information on Change Control Procedures

---

Current Version Date: 10/10/2011

Lab #10 - Worksheet

Mock IT Infrastructure IP Addressing Schema

		Mock IT Infrastructure IP Address Chart			
Router Name	Serial 0/0	Serial 0/1	Fastethernet 0/0	Fastethernet 0/1	Loopback 0
R1.WEST COVINA	172.19.0.2 /30	172.20.0.1 /30	172.20.8.1 /24	172.20.20.1 /24	172.20.1.1 /32
Description	R1.SEATTLE-S 0/1	R1.NORFOLK-S 0/1	DMZ-LAN-SW1-FE0/16	TRUST-LAN-SW2-FE0/16	
Router Name	Serial 0/0	Serial 0/1	Fastethernet 0/0	Fastethernet 0/1	Loopback 0
R1.SEATTLE	172.18.0.2 /30	172.19.0.1 /30	172.19.8.1 /24	172.19.20.1 /24	172.19.1.1 /32
Description	R1.INDY-S 0/1	R1.WESTCOVINA-S 0/0	DMZ-LAN-SW1-F0/2-V400	TRUST-LAN-SW2-F0/2-V401	
Router Name	Serial 0/0	Serial 0/1	Fastethernet 0/0	Fastethernet 0/1	Loopback 0
R1.INDY	172.17.0.2 /30	172.18.0.1 /30	172.18.8.1 /24	172.18.20.1 /24	172.18.1.1 /32
Description	R1.TAMPA-S 0/1	R1.SEATTLE-S 0/0	DMZ-LAN-SW1-F0/17-V300	TRUST-LAN-SW2-F0/17-V301	
Router Name	Serial 0/0	Serial 0/1	Fastethernet 0/0	Fastethernet 0/1	Loopback 0
R1.TAMPA	172.16.0.2 /30	172.17.0.1 /30	172.17.8.1 /24	172.17.20.1 /24	172.17.1.1 /32
Description	R1.NORFOLK-S 0/1	R1.INDY-S 0/0	DMZ-LAN-SW1-F0/7-V200	TRUST-LAN-SW2-F0/7-V201	
Router Name	Serial 0/0	Serial 0/1	Fastethernet 0/0	Fastethernet 0/1	Loopback 0
R1.NORFOLK	172.20.0.2 /30	172.16.0.1 /30	172.16.8.1 /24	172.16.20.1 /24	172.16.1.1 /32
Description	R1.WEST COVINA-S 0/1	R1.TAMPA-S 0/0	DMZ-LAN-SW1-FE0/1	TRUST-LAN-SW2-FE0/1	
Switch Name	Vlan 100	Fastethernet 0/1	Fastethernet 0/2	Fastethernet 0/7	Fastethernet 0/8
LAN.SW1	172.16.8.5 /24				
Description		R1.NORFOLK-F 0/0	R1.SEATTLE-F 0/0	R1.TAMPA-F0/0	R1.WEST COVINA-F0/0
Switch Name	Vlan 101	Fastethernet 0/1	Fastethernet 0/2	Fastethernet 0/7	Fastethernet 0/8
LAN.SW2	172.16.20.5 /24				
Description		R1.NORFOLK-F 0/1	R1.SEATTLE-F 0/1	R1.TAMPA-F0/1	R1.WEST COVINA-F0/1
ASA Name	Vlan2 "Inside"	Vlan501 "Outside"	Vlan600 "DMZ"		
ASA-Student	172.31.0.1 /24 (IP Default GW)	172.20.20.10 /24	172.29.0.2 /24		
Description	Can only ping this from vlan2.	Can ping this from outside.	Cannot ping this from outside.		
ASA Name	Vlan2 "Inside"	Vlan501 "Outside"	Vlan600 "DMZ"		
ASA-Instructor	172.30.0.1 /24 (IP Default GW)	172.20.20.11 /24	172.29.0.1 /24		
Description	Can ony ping this from vlan2.	Can ping this from outside.	Cannot ping this from outside.		

Current Version Date: 10/10/2011

Lab #10 - Assessment Worksheet

Network Management – FCAPS

Course Name & Number: _____

Student Name: _____

Instructor Name: _____

Lab Due Date: _____

Overview

In this lab, studenta will learn how to design and configure an SNMP Fault Management and alarming solution on the Mock IT Infrastructure utilizing Spiceworks. Spiceworks provides a free systems management, inventory and helpdesk software application. Students will learn how to capitalize on all the features of this application as an Asset Management solution and managing SNMP Performance Management. In addition to Implementing Security Management and controls throughout the IP network infrastructure by configuring network monitoring, alerts and email notifications as well as report generation. Students will also become familiar with crafting a Change Control procedure definition for systems administration and organizational management purposes.

Lab Assessment Questions & Answers

1. What is the function of SNMP within the network infrastructure?

2. What kind of software is needed for SNMP reporting and management?

Current Version Date: 10/10/2011

3. What is the command sequence for configuring SNMP on a Cisco 28xx router?

4. What is the significance of "RO" in the command sequence when configuring SNMP logging on a Cisco 29xx Switch?

5. What is displayed in the Inventory >Devices tab of the Spiceworks interface?

6. What is displayed in the Inventory >Network Map tab of the Spiceworks interface?

7. After the offline alerts were configured and the interface links were disconnected what did you observe?

8. In terms of upholding the C.I.A triad, creating SNMP alerts fulfills what aspects of the triad?

Current Version Date: 10/10/2011

9. What are the six (6) stages of a Change Control Procedure?

10. In Stage 3 - Approval, who is responsible for the decision on whether proceed with the proposed change or deny it?

Current Version Date: 10/10/2011

TCP/IP Protocol Primer Cheat Sheet

TCP/IP Protocol Primer & Well-Known Port Numbers

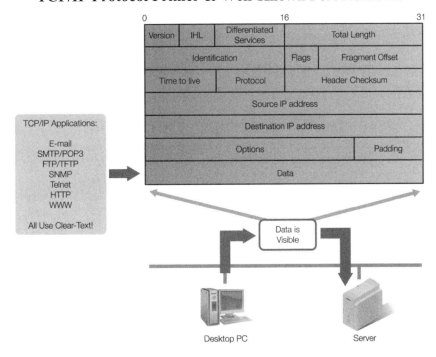

TCP/IP Figure – IP Packet Header & Data Payload Field

FTP	File Transfer Protocol	Port #21
SSH	Secure Shell	Port #22
TELNET	Tele-Network	Port #23
SMTP	Simple Mail Transfer Protocol	Port #25
WHOIS	WHO IS	Port #43
DNS	Domain Name Service	Port #53
DHCP	Dynamic Host Control Protocol	Port #67
TFTP	Trivial File Transfer Protocol	Port #69
HTTP	Hyper Text Transfer Protocol	Port #80
POP3	Post Office Protocol 3	Port #110
SFTP	Secure File Transfer Protocol	Port #115
SNMP	Simple Network Management Protocol	Port #161
HTTPS	Hyper Text Transfer Protocol Secure	Port #443

Current Version Date: 10/10/2011